Numb

Numb

How the Information Age Dulls Our Senses and How We Can Get Them Back

Charles R. Chaffin

WILEY

Library of Congress Cataloging-in-Publication Data:

Names: Chaffin, Charles R., author.
Title: Numb : how the information age dulls our senses and how we can get them back / Charles R. Chaffin.
Description: Hoboken, New Jersey : Wiley, [2021] | Includes bibliographical references and index.
Identifiers: LCCN 2021005107 (print) | LCCN 2021005108 (ebook) | ISBN 9781119774358 (hardback) | ISBN 9781119774495 (adobe pdf) | ISBN 9781119774488 (epub)
Subjects: LCSH: Human information processing. | Distraction (Psychology) | Attention.
Classification: LCC BF444 .C43 2021 (print) | LCC BF444 (ebook) | DDC 153—dc23
LC record available at https://lccn.loc.gov/2021005107
LC ebook record available at https://lccn.loc.gov/2021005108

COVER DESIGN: PAUL MCCARTHY

SKY10026809_050621

*T*o all who have taught me, whether scholars, students, or educators, and others who have fed my wonderment and spirit. To those closest to me – Mom, Dad, Amy, Josh, Cole, Grandma, Kostas, Ryan, Steven, Steven, Gary, Keith, David, Roger, Brian, Richard, Mike, Bob – all of whom bring love, support, and authenticity to my life. To all of the helpers.

Contents

Preface   ix

Acknowledgments   xiii

Introduction   xv

Chapter 1   The Information Age   1

Chapter 2   Can I Have Your Attention Please?   11

Chapter 3   The News   19

Chapter 4   Instagram Worthy   31

Chapter 5   Who's the Pigeon Now?   39

Chapter 6   A Habit of Distraction   47

Chapter 7   Tinder and I Are Registered at Amazon   55

Chapter 8   Confirmation Bias   63

Chapter 9   Compassion Fatigue   73

Chapter 10   Too Much Information   79

Chapter 11   FOMO   87

Contents

Chapter 12 The Outrage Machine   95

Chapter 13 Tribalism   103

Chapter 14 Instant Gratification   111

Chapter 15 Loneliness   119

Chapter 16 Choice   127

Chapter 17 Impulse Buying   135

Chapter 18 Porn   143

Chapter 19 Publisher or Platform?   149

Chapter 20 Algorithms   157

Chapter 21 Regaining the Feeling   167

References   **175**

Index   **189**

Preface

I wrote *Numb* because we have too much to read.

This information age has us constantly plugged in, and yet we are feeling as disconnected as ever. There are a multitude of sources for news and information, yet we struggle to stay informed, as fact is labeled opinion and opinion is labeled as fact. Sensationalism provides a front-row seat to the suffering of others, yet our capacity for compassion for those around us is limited as images of tragedy become routine and conflict becomes the norm. We have more choices than we could ever imagine, everything from colleges to potential mates to brands of mustard. Yet many of us are paralyzed to decide, and in some cases are unhappy and mired in regret over past choices. The number of emails and text messages that we receive on a daily basis can be overwhelming to our Stone Age brains, causing us to struggle to filter the relevant from the irrelevant. Social media promises connection to billions of other humans around the world, yet we struggle with loneliness, tribalism, and FOMO as these platforms lure us into a dopamine loop that provides a short-term fix, sometimes at the expense of authenticity. Algorithms provide us exactly what we want to read, watch, and engage, diminishing our horizons rather than expanding them, while at the same time facilitating a polarized society where common ground is, quite frankly, uncommon. With all of these factors in mind, it is not surprising that the information age is making us numb.

Our attention is both limited and valuable. We only have so much of it at any given time. It is vital, as it drives our consciousness and, ultimately, where and to what we direct our cognitive and physical resources. Given the sea of information and the limits of our attention, we have become overloaded with the sights and sounds that are now a significant part of our everyday lives. Technology lures our attention onto apps of all kinds through push notifications and reward systems that work to engage us and ultimately keep us engaged. The technology and many of our sources of information have different objectives than our own. While the user or viewer is interested in staying informed or connected, social media platforms, streaming services, and cable news channels all have a vested interest in capturing and, perhaps more importantly, keeping our attention. It is not enough to just log on or "tune in." These platforms are designed to keep you engaged for as long as possible, through algorithms that provide similar content based upon past consumption and variable rewards that keep you posting and reposting and checking and rechecking those posts and reposts. Sensationalism and opinion keep viewers engaged through breaking news that may or may not be breaking news and opinion that sometimes only confirms existing biases. Through these tricks and tools, platforms of all kinds deliver screen time and ratings to advertisers, while the user sometimes remains no more informed or connected than before. We are living in an attention economy where this scarce resource has become the price for much of the information that is around us. Social media – an attention marketplace where regular exchanges of this valuable currency take place – also brings those who are seeking attention. Many visit and revisit Facebook, Instagram, and a host of other apps seeking validation from others, whether the subject is a vacation, a new car, or their most recent cheeseburger. These same platforms are a breeding ground for echo chambers and confirmation bias as individuals with similar perspectives come together. In some cases, the loudest or wildest conspiracy theories within the echo chamber receive the most attention, leading to further bias, misinformation, and in some cases radicalization. Whether searching for attention via shirtless selfies or political misinformation, many see social media as a platform for panhandling for attention. This search for attention and validation sometimes comes at the expense of authenticity as we prioritize the rewards of the platform with perfect strangers at the expense of meaning and connection with those closest to us.

There are immense benefits to this information age. It provides incredible power to fuel our abilities to problem solve, create, and even help those who live a world away. Our sustained connectivity fuels almost every aspect of our daily lives. Algorithms help fight crime and enable better medical diagnoses. We have the capabilities to be informed voters and investors, learning about each issue and how it impacts our communities, families, and wallets. There is not only a democratization of information but also a universal ability to express our viewpoints. Social media provides the billions who engage it the ability to convey their lived experience, no matter how trivial or serious. However, with all of those benefits, there are by-products to this information age that have real implications on our ability to experience our environment, think critically, and live our lives to the fullest. Technology, and all of the information that goes along with it, somehow evolved from a tool to get us to our life's destinations to our actual destination. These by-products, which largely focus on the scarcity of our attention as well as the psychological issues that come with all of this information and connectivity, are at the heart of *Numb*.

I wanted *Numb* to have a real purpose in people's lives. It was not enough to identify the problems with this information age, many of which are quite apparent. But rather, I wanted to present real solutions. I interviewed over 60 professionals, ranging from psychologists to researchers to everyday people, to talk about ways that each of us can address many of the challenges that come from this information age. Each of these interviews has been incredibly useful in my own personal journey, and I hope you see the same value as you read. I present research from a variety of fields in a manner that I hope is digestible and relevant and, perhaps most importantly, answers the "so what" of many aspects of our lives. Nowhere in this book do I argue in favor of any type of technology oasis or dopamine fasting where we cut off our access to social media or any other platform or information source. Rather, *Numb* is written to help us use information and technology as a tool to make our lives better. Our smart-phones, PCs, televisions, radios, and all the other devices that help us receive and create information can be useful to us if they are an accompaniment to our lives, rather than the primary focus of our attention.

My vision for *Numb* is a book that can be read cover to cover, with short chapters for attention-scarce readers living in a busy world. I suspect that you will identify with some of the topics and vignettes more than others, but regardless, the book is written with context (i.e., the real world) in mind. After the first read – and as the many devices and sources of information once again work to steal your attention – I hope that *Numb* can be a semi-regular reference; a reminder of how to take control and use technology to accentuate our lives rather than control them. At the end of the day (or perhaps at the end of the book), *Numb* is a guided reflection for each of us to determine our own relationship with this information age. The suggestions shared in this book are designed to empower you to use information, and the positive power and connectivity that can go along with it, towards productivity and authenticity. Now that *Numb* has your attention, let us begin.

Acknowledgments

A special thank you to all of the researchers, clinicians, and everyday people who generously contributed to this book. Each one of them were asked to be part of this project because of their expertise and, perhaps more importantly, their willingness to help others. I hope that each of their voices shines through in this book.

Thank you to the team at Wiley for believing in this project from the very beginning and supporting this vision. It was a long time coming to fruition, and throughout, Wiley was steadfast in their support. I cannot imagine a better creative partner.

Introduction

Our attention impacts our world and our world impacts our attention. With attention comes our awareness. Sometimes focused, sometimes divided, our attention helps us in our work, using our knowledge and skills towards everything from problem solving to creating a safe work environment on a job site. It also brings a focus on those around us, noticing their behavior and appearance, what they say and how they say it. With our attention also comes compassion towards the suffering of our neighbor or those far away. Attention is that critical prerequisite to so many of the thoughts, feelings, and actions that make us human. Being educated, skilled, or even empathetic means little without attention. If our attention is not focused on a conversation, we cannot bring our perspective, expertise, or caring to that dialogue. One could have all of the resources in the world to cure disease, fight hunger, or end wars, but if her attention isn't focused on those problems, those resources are not much use.

Each of us has only so much attention. If we focus on something – whether a sound, sight, smell, or touch – that focus is highlighting something as much as it is blocking other sights or sounds around us. For example, as you read this book, you are focusing on the words on this page at the expense of the sounds of voices around you, the smell of food in the kitchen, or even the feeling of the chair in which you are sitting. Attention is a limited resource, so we have to be selective about what we want to focus. If you have this book open, you cannot focus on the words on this page if you are attending to the sound of the neighbors arguing next door. Given that attention is linked to our consciousness, we have in it a valuable and finite resource that requires careful management. If you do not have control of your attention, someone or something else will take it. Walking through any city or town, you will notice the sights, sounds, and even smells that are clamoring (sometimes literally) for your attention. Advertisers and proprietors large and small all know that if your attention is captured, your wallet may soon follow. They use colorful signs and ads, music, and a host of other tactics to lure your attention to their product. Incidentally, my favorite is Cinnabon. They purposely place those ovens in the front of the store to grab your attention with that delicious cinnamon smell. My wallet indeed follows my attention, which takes me on a path towards deliciousness, followed by an even longer path on the treadmill to compensate for it!

Lots of humans in our lives want our attention, too. Bosses, partners, families, and neighbors all want varying levels of our attention at different times. Some want our attention focused towards our work and others want attention focused on their needs to be heard, touched, and loved. When we focus our attention on people and activities, they tend to go better. Or perhaps better stated, if we do not focus our attention on people and activities, they have a higher likelihood of going much worse. If you do not focus your attention on your spouse or partner for a week or a day or maybe even a moment at dinner, it is likely not going to guarantee a healthy interaction. If you do not focus your attention on your work, the quality of your work will likely suffer as well.

The relationship between attention and this information age is powerful. Technology, and all the information that comes along with it, has created numerous places where we can devote our attention. We can (and do) spend our time fixated on the screens around and with us all day, scrolling through social media feeds, responding to text messages, and swiping left and right to glance at profiles of potential mates. We can binge-watch Netflix, YouTube, and cable news programs, and argue with strangers on Twitter about politics, sports teams, and the best breed of cat to own during a blizzard. Each of these activities can take us down rabbit holes that can kill hours per day. We all seem to receive emails by the dozen. Adobe surveyed 1,000 workers and found that they spend on average close to five hours per day checking email. Five hours looking inside a mailbox! It is rather astounding that given the amount of time that so many of us spend reading, responding, and composing emails that "Outlook Etiquette" isn't part of the interview process for many employment positions. "Do you end your emails with 'Sincerely' or 'Best'? We are really looking for a 'I hope you are well' person to join our team." Oh, and "Read-receipt people need not apply." Nevertheless, each of our emails require our attention to read, process, and respond, knowing full well that there will likely be another email volleyed back like a never-ending tennis match. Whether in our professional or personal lives, our attention is taxed constantly in this information age. Making sense of it all, deciding what is relevant and what isn't, as well as prioritizing what is important, is an art and science in and of itself. Essentially, this information age expands the possibilities of places for us to spend our attention.

Beyond the cognitive aspects associated with the information age, I spent a great deal of time reflecting upon the nature of experience. I started to question what was authentic and what was not. This is not just a commentary relative to fake news, although that is certainly part of it and addressed in this book. I was thinking more about authenticity when it comes to our life experiences, from what gives us joy and happiness to how and if we are truly present with the people and experiences that make up daily life. Picking up my smartphone at dinner to get that dopamine fix via social media meant that I wasn't really present with that friend sitting across the table from me. Is that dopamine hit that comes from the push notification or the attention that comes from a "like" on social media really an authentic experience? In his book *The Necessity of Experience*, Edward Reed identifies ecological information as the type of information that "all humans acquire from their environment through looking, listening, feeling, sniffing, and tasting." Essentially, Reed describes ecological information as things we experience "for ourselves." He identifies the power that ecological information has in engaging with other human beings, including reading their facial expressions, listening carefully to the tone of their voice, and all of the other verbal, nonverbal, and visual signs that accompany our engagement and shared experiences with other human beings. Through technology and this age of information, we see a shift in focus to processed information, which Reed defines as secondhand: signs and symbols based upon our primary experience with one another. These secondhand experiences, whether via television, social media, porn, or any other experience that is conveyed to us by others, has become more dominant than experiencing the world firsthand for ourselves. We seem to be spending an increasing amount of time hearing or viewing the experiences of others rather than participating ourselves. When we think about the idea of FOMO – fear of missing out – it is no wonder that so many of us experience it because we spend a lot of time in the audience observing others. Maybe we are actually missing out!

We all experience the benefits of this information age, from connecting with others across multiple geographic regions to the accessibility of information, whether news, education, or Wikipedia. Information, and the technology that goes along with it, makes our lives better. We have seen during the COVID-19 pandemic an ability for some of us to keep working and at least engaging on some level with those we care for most, even if remotely. However, over the course of the last several years (even prior to the pandemic), I started questioning the impact of this information age on many aspects of our lives. I began reflecting on the relationship between information and my biases, habits, and even participation in echo chambers. I started to wonder how we have all of this information at our fingertips (or in our pockets), and yet we seem to be increasingly less informed. I started thinking about the potential impact of our compassion for those closest to us when we are regularly exposed to graphic images of the suffering of others from far away. With the increasing number of choices available to us, I wondered about our ability to navigate so many options, whether choosing a jar of jam or a life partner? I also began to realize the impact of loneliness on people of all ages and questioned how this was possible when social media was such a big part of our lives. The hours per day that we spend on our smartphones scrolling and texting are immense. At the risk of sounding overly dramatic, what happens at the end of our lives when we look back on all of this time? Will we see this engagement as authentic and enhancing our in-person experiences or will we see it as a waste of time, providing short-term satisfaction at the expense of long-term goals and relationships? The answer for each of us is likely different. For me, it seemed as if there was something missing from this engagement. The short-term dopamine hit was coming at the expense of authentic engagement. The regular access to all the hyperbole, hysteria, and echo chambers began to numb me, making me feel overwhelmed with emotion. Compassion fatigue is only one component of this short yet broad work, but it was the genesis of this book. I began to reflect that the emotion I was feeling from information on the screen was creating a level of apathy in my real life. Essentially, I was hearing about bad news and suffering all day viewing the news and social media, so I didn't need more of it in real life. Real life is where I can make a difference. Real life is the people who are closest to me whom I care about. I needed to better understand this phenomenon so I could be present with them. I wanted authenticity.

That brings us to *Numb*. My objective with this book was to better understand, and then ultimately outline, the pushes and pulls on our attention in this information age. Perhaps more importantly, I wanted to outline some of the psychological factors that are created through this information age and its impact on our attention. And finally, what is the "so what?" of all of this, meaning what can we do about it to make our lives better in some way, shape, or form? Although *Numb* is not a novel by any means, it does tell a story of how we so often become engrossed in technology looking for love through likes, swipes, and a host of other bells and whistles. In many cases, we constantly return to social media and many other apps looking for love, attention, and recognition only to fail at finding it. We become addicted to that pursuit, through dopamine loops and habits. If we are not careful, we can find ourselves looking for love from social media, apps, and devices that will never love us back. As you will see with many of the topics, there is an ongoing "chicken or egg" here, where it is unclear whether those who are lonely or struggling with choice are more attracted to their devices or whether time on these devices facilitates loneliness and many of the other factors mentioned throughout the book. If you are looking for a quick answer that summarizes the book, there isn't one (I am not sure I would tell if there was; why read further if the mystery is solved in the introduction?). However, I do think that if you have been thinking about your own relationship with technology and in particular, this information age, you may identify with some of the vignettes and research shared and decide for yourself how it all may be impacting you. I hope that the clinical psychologists, therapists, researchers, and everyday people who were interviewed as part of this book bring value to observation, relevance to research, and hopefully solutions to problems. I am grateful to each of them for their contributions in helping this book become a potential resource. I personally found their insights incredibly helpful to me in my journey towards living in this information age. I hope you will, too.

So let us begin. I hope that *Numb* satisfies some curiosities when it comes to many of the experiences we all seem to have in this information age. We can be connected and engaged with information without letting it eliminate the authentic experiences that are so important to being human. We can develop ways to eliminate habits that are not serving our long-term goals and interests. One of the primary themes that seems to emerge throughout the book is the notion that information and technology are at their best when they are tools to something greater. It can bring new experiences and people into our lives in meaningful ways. If managed properly, this information age can help us be more objective and well-informed regarding issues that affect both us and our communities. The possibilities are endless. It is just a matter of balance, understanding, and empowerment. As you read *Numb*, I invite you to reflect upon your own experiences in your daily life and decide what's working for you and what isn't – and perhaps ultimately, what needs to change. I hope that *Numb* empowers you to take control of your attention and use it towards what you think is important, authentic, and fulfilling. We just have to find ways to manage all the information and technology around us, rather than all of it managing us.

The Information Age

Josh is facing a pretty normal Tuesday. The alarm on his smart-phone rings at 7 a.m. and as soon as he turns it off, he immediately starts exploring his social media newsfeeds. One Facebook friend posted a picture of a sloppy Big Mac that he ate at McDonald's; another posted that she did not like the newest Netflix series (but is binge-watching it nonetheless), and Josh's cousin shared a political rant predicting the end of the republic (again). Josh then questions his own selfie on Instagram and wonders if he should have used a fil-ter; it had been two days and not many "likes." He wonders whether he should take it down. Has his ex seen the picture? Does it look like he's gained weight? Josh then gets lost in a scroll of Instagram posts from friends as well as a slew of strangers whom he follows. He explores all of the vacation pictures that several friends posted and wonders why he hasn't had a vacation like that in years. He asks himself, "How do they find the time and money to travel around the world like that? I wish that were me."

As a part of his daily routine getting ready for work, Josh lis-tens to the morning news in the background to hear the traffic and weather reports. Another accident on the freeway means either an alternate trip or a late arrival to the office. He asks himself whether he should skip breakfast to make up some of the time. His mind returns to the selfie. Maybe skipping breakfast would be a good idea if he has gained weight. He thinks briefly about what an exercise regimen might look like. He hates running and wonders how much a gym membership might cost. Josh's attention shifts back to the news, where he hears about the pain and suffering from yesterday's typhoon in the Pacific as well as the latest drama unfolding on the set of *The Bachelor*. He hears the latest report on the market and wonders briefly about the status of his 401(k) and when and if he will be able to retire. He wonders how much longer he can work, and how much longer he wants to work at his current job. Throughout, his attention on the news of the day is intermittent as his mind also wanders to a wide range of topics. Does his youngest really need braces? Should he get a haircut? How should he approach today's meeting with his team?

Upon arrival at the office (he was 15 minutes late), Josh sees dozens of emails that require his attention. He thumbs through each of them, getting a sense of the topics and determining which may be a priority. He has no time to respond to any of them as he begins to tackle a packed Tuesday agenda. His first meeting had two interruptions from staff members who needed a decision regarding a completely unrelated topic. Josh shifted his attention quickly to make the urgent decision before returning his focus to the content of the meeting. As his colleague shared some of her ideas regarding a new project, Josh's mind wandered back to one of the two decisions he just made, reflecting upon whether it was the right choice or not. He misses some of what his team member is saying during his reflection. As he focuses back on what she is saying, his phone vibrates with a push notification of a text from his youngest daughter. He fights the urge to read the text during the meeting. His mind then wandered as he considered why she could possibly be texting so early in the day. Was she sick? Was it another issue in her biology class? He focuses his attention back to the meeting, nodding his head to indicate that he is paying attention even as text messages and reflections have taken his attention away. Josh's day continues with meetings and rare appearances in his workspace, which also brings with it several interruptions from both his boss and co-workers, all of whom need something from him right away. Josh stares at his voluminous email inbox sporadically but spends little time reading and responding as his attentional focus switches from person to person, meeting to meeting, and push notification to push notification. By the end of the day, Josh has little time to develop the two reports that are due by the end of the week. Each time he begins to work on them, someone comes to his desk with a question, derailing his attention, and in some cases taking his work down an unexpected rabbit hole.

Josh's only companion throughout the entire day is his smartphone. It is on the table in front of him during meetings, in his hand when walking to lunch, and next to him while he is at his desk. He averages about three to four hours of screen time per day. Sometimes he checks his phone to respond to a text message and sometimes he is reading a push notification via one of the news apps. As with his email inbox, he also has a tendency to scroll mindlessly through the endless newsfeed on social media between meetings and phone calls. Whether at work or at home, Josh will check his social media apps after posting something to see if anyone has responded and sometimes he picks up his phone to see if he has those three tiny bubbles that indicate a response to his text is forthcoming. And sometimes he checks his cell phone for no real reason. If his phone vibrates, Josh responds by at least looking at his screen, indicating that at least some portion of his attention is regularly focused on the device, even if it is facedown.

Many of our days are not unlike Josh's. We are all living within a tidal wave of information and it is seemingly coming from all angles. Just within the environment around us, our brains are absorbing everything that our senses have to offer, whether sights, sounds, smells, or touch. We focus on the speech of those around us, deciphering their meaning and (hopefully) communicating an adequate verbal and nonverbal response. Internal and external distractions bring with them additional information requiring us to sift through each to determine what is meaningful and worthy of a response. Through technology, we have access to 24-hour news cycles that are constantly racing to bring breaking news, sensationalized videos, and mountains of opinion. The scandals and tragedies, each of which get their short 15 minutes of fame, seem to become more and more vividly detailed as competing news sources race not only to be the first, but perhaps to be the most shocking. Before the beginning of the commercial break comes the pull to keep you engaged, asking questions that once again raise an internal alarm of some sort. "Is America dying a slow and gruesome death before our very eyes? Find out in 90 seconds." How can we turn away? I have to know if America is going to be happy and healthy. Routinely, a 10-minute commitment to catch up on the day's news turns into 45 minutes of sensationalism, opinions, and sometimes outrage – and I am not sure they ever mentioned what will happen to America after the commercial break!

On social media, we engage, post, and retweet regularly, hoping for the likes and comments that seem so prized. Instagram has created a virtual sweatshop of people diligently working to select just the right selfie with the perfect filter. We perform the endless scroll on Facebook to observe the curated lives of our friends while we curate our own lives for them. Within the past several years, many of us have developed the habit of doomscrolling, perusing our social media newsfeed for what we expect will be more bad news. It can become a regular diet of news regarding political turmoil, and economic and racial inequality, maybe garnished with a pandemic for good measure. We engage and reengage those within our echo chambers, receiving confirmation of our positions. Like those seeking attention through selfies, many within the echo chambers stretch the boundaries of the truth, using less than credible sources to gain affirmation within their tribe. The wildest conspiracy theories sometimes garner the highest amount of attention. In response, the algorithms serve us up more of it, basing new content in our newsfeeds upon what we have previously engaged.

Through the use of algorithms, YouTube recommends millions of videos to users based upon our previous viewing habits. As a platform that allows users to post content that has little to no vetting process, there is something for just about every mainstream and radicalized belief. With so many videos, the algorithms on YouTube are like a good waiter at an all-you-can-eat pancake breakfast: serving you up more of exactly what you want, without judgment. We engage and reengage on social media for that dopamine high of receiving both new information as well as attention that comes in the form of likes and comments. We spend hours per day, logged in and sharing curated aspects of our lives, to get that dopamine hit and perhaps also searching for connectivity with others. There is a sad irony that billions of us are connected, yet so many feel isolated and alone. In many cases, we turn to social media for connection, sacrificing many forms of authenticity that come from shared experiences and deeper connections with friends and loved ones.

We generate more data than ever. According to the Data Never Sleeps 5.0 Report, from 2016 to 2018, we created 90% of all of the data ever created in the world in just two years. Every day, 1.5 billion people are on Facebook. Every second, 456,000 tweets and over four million YouTube videos are viewed. Every minute, we send 16 million text messages, swipe on Tinder close to one million times, and send over 150 million emails. Not long ago, the limits to our ability to create, learn, and experience were limited by a dearth of information. Now, in this information age, we are limited by our cognitive capacity to comprehend all of the information that is available to us on a daily basis. Networks, laptops, and smartphones have all evolved to have more capacity, with one notable exception: our brains. We are still functioning with the same brains that our ancestors used thousands of years ago for hunting and procreating and then hunting and procreating some more. With the expanded capacity of technology and all of the information that comes along with it, there is an incredible battle for perhaps your most prized possession: your attention.

A Scarcity of Attention

When I think of all the things in our world that compete for our attention, the first place that comes to mind is Times Square. It is a battlefield for attention where billboards are stacked upon one another using a variety of colors and flashing lights. There is flickering, neon, and other forms of luminescence all selling something, from Broadway shows to hamburgers and fancy red cars. These signs are positioned within every possible inch of our sightlines, all with the purpose of drawing our thoughts to their product or experience. Of course, I cannot forget the people dressed as furry cartoon characters that invite you to take a picture (yes, I have done it and there is photographic evidence of such an experience). But if you have had the opportunity to walk through Times Square, you might remember how difficult it was to focus on any one particular sign or activity. You could be fixated on an ad on a high-definition screen but then suddenly become fixated on an even brighter set of lights. During the entire experience, you are likely focusing your attention on a variety of different sights and sounds, sometimes within the same second. Actually, you might walk away from Times Square and not be able to recall any of the individual ads or signs because there were so many stimuli and it was difficult to process any one particular item.

Most of our daily lives do not look anything like Times Square, but think of all of the activities, devices, and information sources that you come into contact with every day that, like those neon signs, all compete for your attention in one way or another. In his morning routine, Josh was devoting his attention towards multiple activities simultaneously. He has dressed himself for work many, many times and so therefore it requires very little thought or attention. He could get dressed while listening to the news or thinking about his day ahead. However, what if for the first time, he had to tie a bow tie? He might have difficulty listening to the weather while simultaneously focusing his attention on making that first perfect knot. Since it is a new (and complex) task, the bow tie would require additional attention that would take away from his ability to concentrate on anything else. In this case, Josh might ignore the news or even turn off the TV so he could focus on his bow tie. Attention is a zero-sum game because we have only so much to give. If all of our attention is devoted to doing something, we cannot "dig deeper" and find more for something else. The popular analogy of our attention acting as a bucket of water is apt: every cup or spoonful of water that we take out leaves us less in the bucket, or in the case of attention, less to devote elsewhere to other things. So, if the amount of human attention is fixed, it is valuable, perhaps every bit as valuable as any other resource we can offer any other person or activity.

Herbert Simon, the Nobel Prize–winning economist and cognitive psychologist, was one of the first to articulate the basis for an attention economy. He suggested that "a wealth of information creates a scarcity of what that information consumes," which is attention. Essentially, we pay for items not necessarily with money but with our attention. Websites and apps lure us to visit or stay on their platforms with catchy animations or lots of information crowded into one site, hoping that something will catch our eye and get us clicking further. With almost universal access to the internet, there is a wealth of information that is both free and accessible. At the same time, our cognitive capacity has not changed. Therefore, we have to make decisions regarding where we devote our attention.

Speaking of decisions, the buffet line at almost any Las Vegas casino is a fabulous place. These colossal gardens of gluttony offer nearly every type of food imaginable. However, our plates – and our stomachs – have only so much capacity. We cannot possibly consume all of the food that is available to us, so we have to make decisions. We can certainly sample a little bit of a lot of things, but we cannot expect to consume everything. Therefore, since we cannot have it all, we have to prioritize what we want, or perhaps need, the most. Like our plates and stomachs at the buffet, our cognitive capacity is limited. We have to consciously make decisions regarding the information we consume at any given time, filtering what we want and need from what we don't. Incidentally, making healthy choices for both information and buffets requires immense self-discipline – and sometimes antacids afterwards!

What are your goals for today? What is it that you want to accomplish? Is there something that you want to experience, whether connecting with a close friend or feeling the burn of a great workout? What about your long-term goals for yourself? Is it advancing in your career or developing deeper connections with those around you? Do you want to rebuild that old car that your father owned? Perhaps learn a musical instrument? We all have short- and long-term goals for ourselves that relate to our personal and professional lives. In some cases, barriers to meeting those goals might be a shortage of time or money. It might be related to raising children, a new job, or caring for an aging parent. However, in many cases, the biggest hurdle to our goals is merely distraction. For me, I began to realize that technology was a big distraction: the 10, 20, or 30 times a day that I was mindlessly picking up my smartphone to scroll through a newsfeed or fire up the Twitter outrage machine. Initially, I thought that the reason why I wasn't reaching some of my goals was the usual "not enough time" or "things are busy at work." As time went on, I began to reflect upon where I was devoting my attention and found that where I was investing much of it was wasteful. At the surface, it isn't that devoting enormous amounts of attention towards social media or another information platform is good or bad. Rather, it is up for debate for each of us as to whether they are consistent or inconsistent with our goals. As we all know, there is never enough time and life is always busy. However, things can seem a lot busier when you're fighting a consistent distraction that is with you almost all of the time. For me, mindlessly picking up my phone for no apparent reason came at a price. That price was my attention on the things that mattered most to me. It only occurred to me when the goals I created for myself, both professionally and personally, weren't being realized.

By-Products of This Information Age

At the risk of stating the obvious, the goals for the technology around us are not consistent with our own personal goals. Media outlets – through nonstop news coverage and clickbait headlines – are designed to lure us onto their channels and sites. Social media has a vested interest in keeping you on their platforms for as long as possible through the use of algorithms and clever little "rewards" that we will discuss later in the book. We engage in our newsfeeds or the endless recommended videos on YouTube at the expense of many of our short- and long-term goals. Echo chambers and outrage machines keep us emotionally vested in content that we post and engage. When it comes to social media platforms, as Mark Weinstein describes it, "We are not the users, we are the product." The realization that something you engage routinely is not aligned with your goals is obvious but also important. Think about other technology around us. Our cars, washing machines, and microwaves are all designed to meet our goals, whether it's transportation or popping popcorn. Our smartphones, and all of the apps that go along with it, are not the same. They have important functions in our daily lives, but it is not as simple as giving us what we both want and need to live our best lives. There is at best a Venn diagram between our goals and theirs with a definite yet small crossover. It is not a complete alignment.

Averaging close to four hours of screen time a day, we have become reliant upon social media as a primary outlet to engage others, some of whom we know and some we don't. This connection through technology is valuable when it accompanies in-person relationships, but is isolating if it is our primary vehicle for engagement with others. When we connect in person, whether with a colleague or a friend, we witness the facial expressions and the vocal inflections that come from the dialogue. The processed element of connecting via instant message lacks authenticity, leaving those who stay online for hours per day isolated. In many respects, technology places us in a bubble that we carry with us, isolating us from the people around us and limiting authentic interactions with new people. In her book *Alone Together*, MIT professor Sherry Turkle states, "a train station (like an airport, a café, or a park) is no longer a communal space but a place of social collections. People come together but do not speak to each other. Each is tethered to a mobile device and to the people and places to which that device serves as a portal." Ironically, our constant connection in some respect makes us more disconnected, even when surrounded by other humans, potentially other lonely humans.

The sensationalism that comes from news exposes us to the suffering of others on a daily, if not hourly, basis. This makes the act of viewing suffering mundane, creating potential compassion fatigue. The echo chambers that are created within social media impact not only how we view important issues as voters and citizens, but also how we engage and treat one another. We also face an onslaught of daily decisions via technology. We have become overwhelmed with choice, whether it is in the dairy aisle or on Tinder. How do we navigate all these options without becoming incapacitated? Given the ability of our smartphones to lure us into a habit of scrolling, how do we develop a well-balanced diet of social media without it limiting other aspects of our lives? What about tribalism, sensationalism, FOMO, outrage, confirmation bias, and a host of other factors that confront us every day in this information age? We seem aware, yet uninformed and polarized. Outraged, yet apathetic. When I think of all of the push and pull of our attention that comes from this information and perhaps most importantly, the psychological impacts of all of it, the word that always comes front of mind is *numb*.

The sports broadcaster Beano Cook once said, "Life in the 1960s was far better, with three notable exceptions: Medicine, civil rights, and air conditioning." Although certainly clever with some truth to it, life today has many benefits beyond the three he mentioned. This age of information brings with it numerous possibilities. We have the ability to communicate with people from every corner of the globe who bring different worldviews and perspectives to important topics as well as our own life. Medical breakthroughs can be achieved through online collaboration and dissemination to a broad group of scientists. Look no further than the COVID-19 pandemic to see the benefit of large-scale international medical collaborations that could only be advanced through this information age. We have the ability to be better-informed consumers, voters, worshippers, and professionals through our access to information. It is a matter of finding the right balance of accessing information that makes our lives better, engaging enough of the news to be well-informed, and connecting with social media in both a positive and genuine way. The solution to meeting all of our short- and long-term goals is not eliminating all of our technology. Rather, it is finding the right balance with information and technology in our personal and professional lives. Each of us has to decide if this information age really and truly makes our lives better. Perhaps there are tweaks you can make in your relationship with social media, cable news, or dating apps. You might have initially engaged social media or dating apps thinking they would be useful to become more connected. Has that goal been achieved? Have you been realizing that lately you have become too connected? I hope the insight from this book, and the reflective process that goes along with it, will help you answer those questions and find the right balance. I hope that it is a worthwhile journey.

CHAPTER 2

Can I Have Your Attention Please?

Imagine that you are driving a car down the road. You are effortlessly moving down your path, maneuvering the steering wheel
through the twists and turns as well as hitting the accelerator and
brake when necessary. You have driven on this road dozens of times
so you know each curve and even a few potholes. As you are driving,
your attention shifts from the road to an important meeting that is
happening at work on Monday morning. As you continue your trip,
you think about the work that needs to be done in advance of that
meeting. By the end of the 20-minute drive, you have mapped out
how you would like the Monday meeting to flow and even considered how you would like to structure the presentation.

Now imagine that you are driving down the same road and you
have a passenger sitting next to you. She is a good friend who is sharing the emotional details of her recent breakup. You are performing
all of the same tasks in driving the car as outlined above but also
listening and responding to your friend's story. You are constantly
shifting focus between the road and your friend, sometimes focusing
on the road a bit more when there is a turn and sometimes concen-
trating on your friend when she gets more emotional or asks you a

11

question. Your mind briefly wanders to the Monday meeting while she is talking, but between the road and your friend, there is little opportunity to focus on the flow of the upcoming presentation or potential outcomes. As you drive, you are responding to your friend with an occasional "yes" or "no" or even a head nod while your eyes are focused on the road. By the end of the drive, you have a clear sense of what happened in your friend's breakup (or at least her side of the story), but nothing beyond a reminder that the Monday presentation needs some work.

Just for fun, let's add one more scenario. It is now pouring rain while you are driving: Same road, same friend, same breakup. You are struggling to see the road while steering and carefully managing the accelerator. Given the severity of the road conditions, you prioritize your attention towards driving. You are using the brake far more often as the rainstorm impedes the view of the road ahead of you. Very little of your attention is devoted to your friend's breakup story; you only manage to perceive when she gets more emotional. You are mindful enough to offer a few grunts of agreement while she talks, but in reality if you had to recount the story of her breakup to others, you would not perform well. Between the white-knuckle driving and your friend's breakup story, you never once thought of your presentation at the Monday meeting.

All of these different scenarios highlight the nature of attention. In the first example, you were familiar with the road and the conditions were ideal for driving. You did not have to concentrate too heavily on the path ahead so you had attention to devote to the meeting on Monday. You were able to develop some concrete plans for the presentation in your mind that will be useful when you return to your desk. In the second scenario, you had attention to devote to your friend's breakup story because the drive was not overly taxing. However, between the drive and your friend, you had little attention to devote to the planning of the Monday presentation. In this scenario, you were compelled to allocate whatever attention you had left over from driving to your friend. Because the road was clear, you could devote attention to your friend's breakup story. However, in the third scenario, when the conditions of the road became dangerous with the storm, you had to prioritize your attention towards driving and limit how much attention you could devote to your friend with almost none dedicated to your Monday presentation.

What Is Attention?

Attention is one of those terms that we throw around often. We ask for others' attention. It is asked of us and, in some cases, it is taken away from us through a variety of means. If you ask 100 people the meaning of the word "attention," you are likely to get dozens of different answers. You would hear words like "concentration" and "focus" but also words that associate attention with the senses such as seeing, hearing, and feeling. Even among psychologists there are a number of different perspectives regarding the actual meaning. William James, in *Principles of Psychology* wrote, "Everyone knows what attention is. It is the taking possession by the mind in clear and vivid form, of one out of what seem several simultaneously possible objects or trains of thought. . . . It implies withdrawal from some things in order to deal effectively with others, and is a condition which has a real opposite in the confused, dazed, scatterbrained state."

At a more basic level, attention is how we select information in the environment around us. Many visualize attention like a highlighter on the page, where you are focusing mental energy on particular words. Jason McCarley, a cognitive psychologist at Oregon State University, describes attention as "the thread through all of our awareness." As he puts it, if we do not attend to something, we don't perceive it. Thinking back to the driving example, if we are focused intently on driving the car in a heavy rainstorm, we may be able to perceive that our friend is talking but not really have any comprehension of the details of her story. (We might even ask her to wait for the story until the storm clears.) As McCarley puts it, "attention is the gateway to our consciousness. Without attending to something, whether a sound, sight, or other, we cannot be conscious of its existence." One of the most famous experiments to illustrate this effect was the Invisible Gorilla experiment. Chris Chabris and Daniel Simons asked viewers to count the number of times players passed a basketball among themselves. In the meantime, a person dressed in a gorilla suit appeared in the center of the image. Viewers often failed to see the person in the gorilla suit because their attention was focused on the students passing the basketball. This study, one of the most famous in psychology, demonstrated focusing on one thing can come at the expense of focusing on other items. In this case, the viewers' attention was concentrated on the players and they were not conscious of the existence of the person in the gorilla suit.

We see this manifest itself in many parts of modern life. Magicians manipulate people's attention from one location to another, asking audience members to focus on one location at the expense of elsewhere (usually their other hand) where objects are hidden and reappear elsewhere.

We only have so much attention at any given time. Where we allocate it is of vital importance. As you read this chapter, you are devoting your attention to the words on this page, making meaning out of the string of the text that makes sentences and ultimately paragraphs of thoughts and ideas. But what else is happening while you are reading? Are you sitting on your couch reading while the TV or stereo is playing? Are there voices around you that you are tuning out in order to make sense of what you are reading? If you began to focus on the sounds around you while reading, your comprehension would likely decrease dramatically. Your eyes may move along the words, but you may not get any meaning out of what is written. Attention, therefore, is as much about what you tune out as what you focus on. As James stated, attention "implies withdrawal from some things in order to deal effectively with others." Our smartphones are a prime example. Whether we are texting while driving (please don't), during meetings, or while on a date, we are allocating attention towards our phone at the expense of what is occurring around us. We may think that we are successfully focusing on both items at once, but engaging our environment in any substantive way while focusing on whatever you are texting is almost impossible. You can give a few grunts to your dinner companion while they are sharing a story with you during your texts, but it is unlikely that you have enough attention to really focus on and comprehend what they are saying. Of course, if you continue texting (phubbing, if you will), you may find yourself spending the rest of the evening alone with your phone. Our ability to control our attention is invaluable in this information age. Each of us is trying to do our jobs, run errands, maintain relationships, and experience all of the other chores and joys of life while we are inundated with information and technology designed specifically to distract us. As we will discuss throughout this book, this technology is designed to steal your attention for as many hours as possible. Whether smartphones, TV, or radio, technology is vying for our attention with the goal of redeeming it towards advertising revenue. Apps and tech developers employ a number of strategies to maximize our attention and keep us engaged on their app, site, or device. There is a very real battle for our attention and, given its importance in our daily lives, the stakes are high.

In 1997, Michael Goldhaber suggested that the global economy was shifting from a materials-based economy to one that was attention-based. The currency in this economy is attention. In the digital age, there is no shortage of information. It is everywhere, with everyone contributing to it. There are obviously varying degrees of utility for some of this information, but as Goldhaber suggests, economy is based upon what is scarce and information is not scarce in the least. What is scarce is attention. There are times when we need attention and times when we decide to give attention. As babies, we need attention from our parents for basic survival because we are not yet able to take care of ourselves. As adults, we strive for attention as we attempt to navigate a job or career to support our basic needs. As Goldhaber puts it, with attention from others comes all of the material items that we normally associate with elements of success. For example, with the attention of a community, you can encourage park rehabilitation or voter registration. It isn't that your message or whatever product you are designing and developing is not important. Rather, it's that none of that matters if attention from others is not paid. We pay with our attention on our smartphones every day. We sit through advertising on apps if we do not want to pay an extra fee (that's me when it comes to Words with Friends) and at a more fundamental level, we dedicate our attention to technology at the expense of many other aspects of our lives. Given that attention is a valuable commodity that each of us possesses (with only a finite amount available), attention is being paid – and it is a high price.

Jason McCarley suggests that technology impacts our attentional focus for two basic reasons. First, it compromises our performance. As he describes it, cognitively demanding tasks, by definition, place heavy demands on working memory. Imagine preparing a meal and having to follow a new recipe. During each step of the process, you are constantly checking the ingredients and instructions and then holding that information in your working memory while searching for the ingredient in the pantry or refrigerator. Interruptions displace information from our working memory. So once we are done responding to the interruption, we have to remember what we were doing and recover the information we were holding in our working memory. This is called a resumption lag, which is the time between when the interruption ends and when the primary task resumes. This is a time cost. In addition, as he describes it, these interruptions can also cause errors in our primary tasks. In a worst case, we may entirely neglect to complete some component of the primary task after interruption with potentially dramatic consequences. Interruptions during a pre-flight checklist increase the risk of pilot error, and interruptions to physicians in emergency rooms can lead to medical error.

Second, there is a great deal of stress involved in ignoring all of the distractions that we receive from technology. Think about all of the push notifications, sounds, and vibrations that come from texts, apps, email, and a host of other sources. If you are focusing your attention on a task, there is a great deal of stress in ignoring your smartphone while working on a project or even during a conversation with a friend over coffee. The stress in ignoring the sights and sounds around us can impact performance in a big way. In 1982, students at Public School 98 in New York were subjected to the daily noise of a nearby subway train. The train rumbled past 15 times per day, causing disruptions to the class. After numerous complaints, the Transit Authority cushioned the rails with rubber pads while the Board of Education installed sound-absorbing materials in the classrooms. All of these efforts limited the distractions from the train, and in the years that followed, students' reading levels improved one full grade level. This is by no means a profound revelation: Students do better in school when there are not loud noises occurring throughout the day to distract them. However, the same can be said of all of us as adults: We perform better in our work and social lives when we are not constantly disrupted throughout the day. It may not be as consistently loud as the 1 train to the Bronx, but a distraction is a distraction.

Technology and Our Attention

There is a relationship between technology and attention spans as well. In 2015, Microsoft examined the attention spans of hundreds of volunteers through both EEG scans (electroencephalogram, used to track and record brain waves) and survey data. Microsoft determined that the average attention span was approximately eight seconds, down from 12 seconds in 2000 (Perhaps more shocking, that eight-second average is one second less than the average attention span of a goldfish). Subjects who had digital devices tended to have more difficulty in focusing their attention, particularly those who are constantly switching their attention between short activities. These short activities could be texting while responding to work emails as your attention is switched back and forth between two devices and two distinctly different topics. Many of these attributes are similar to those diagnosed with ADHD (attention deficit hyperactivity disorder), where individuals have difficulty focusing their attention for long periods of time.

The impact of regular distractions certainly adds up. A study from the University of California-Irvine found that after an interruption, it takes on average 23 minutes and 15 seconds to get back on task in a natural work environment. That is, of course, assuming there are no further distractions during that 23 minutes. Those distractions do not just impact our work, but they also impact our focus on our relationships, reflection, and a myriad of other tasks that we perform in our daily lives. Nir Eyal, in his book *Indistractable*, outlines the internal and external triggers that can cause us to lose focus. Internal triggers are the urge to go onto social media or check if someone is texting us (you know, the three bubbles), or Google something just for the sake of googling it. External triggers are the push notifications that come from our smartphones, alerting us to everything from new tweets from the Kardashians to news and information from every app imaginable. We have become so focused on them that they are having an impact on almost every aspect of our daily lives. In fact, a recent study suggests that 10% of people check their smartphones during sex. I will resist the urge to opine on any impact on sexual productivity here, but the point is that we have a challenge when it comes to being focused in our daily lives.

Given that attention is both a vital and a finite resource, we have to take steps to ensure that we are allocating it towards the activities that are most important to us. First, we can actively manage the alerts on our smartphones. Do you really need all of those push notifications? If you cannot part with all of them, then maybe there can be a dedicated time when the smartphone can go into a drawer or even be turned off. At work, having your email open where push notifications alert you to every new email can also be a constant distraction. A dedicated time to focus on email can be a huge boost to productivity. And related, make commitments to complete tasks for a given period of time or even to completion. If you say, "I am going to work on this project for the next hour uninterrupted," then create the environment to do so and get it done. Regardless of the strategy you employ, you are empowered to actively manage any distractions, whether internal or external, to your personal and professional life.

CHAPTER

The News

"The primary purpose of journalism is to provide citizens with the information they need to be free and self-governing."
— Bill Kovach and Tom Rosenstiel, *The Elements of Journalism*

It seems as if there are countless sources for news, including broadcast and cable channels, radio, newspapers, and online platforms, much of which can be accessed directly or via social media. Within each medium, we have to decide which source is trustworthy and which is not, separating fact from opinion and seeking and objectivity over bias. Much of the news draws us to the sensational, prioritizing the graphic over the detail, and in some cases the flashy over substance. In addition, we all have an innate desire for vindication of our opinions, leading us to sources that provide commentary that lends itself to confirmation bias. And if that is not enough, the fast pace of today's news cycle makes the stories that have yet to achieve even their 15 minutes of fame already obsolete, as breaking news headlines suddenly replace the previous ones. As I write this chapter, there are fires blazing through the western part of the United States; two hurricanes threatening the Gulf Coast; an endless carnival of accusations, conspiracy theories, and polls related to the 2020 election; heightened worry about nuclear testing in North Korea; and, not to be outdone, a worldwide pandemic. Each of these stories brings a constant stream of breaking news alerts, push notifications, and opinions. The news today seems like a salad tossed with headline fatigue, information overload, confirmation bias, and way too much sensationalism dressing. The news can be overwhelming.

Our main sources of news have evolved over the past many decades. In the 1960s, network news was considered separate and apart from the entertainment division. Profitable networks thought that a well-funded and respected news division would help both with their reputation as well as mitigate any regulatory pressures from the government. At that time, network news was not designed to make a profit. And yet visibility was high. Walter Cronkite, anchor of the CBS Evening News from the 1960s to the 1980s, was voted "the most trusted man in America." At the same time, local news and newspapers were thriving, representing their cities and regions and cornering the market on commercial and print advertising revenue.

The news landscape changed radically in the 1980s as cable news grew in stature and media conglomerates began taking ownership of the broadcast networks. With this new ownership came a bigger focus on profit within the news divisions. By the 1990s, advertising became more targeted and the audiences for network news were beginning to erode with the increased competition from cable news. In the 2000s, the internet began its assault on newspaper circulation, while social media platforms launched to create an even more competitive environment. Today, according to the Pew Research Center, 49% of Americans get their news from television, with social media now outpacing newspapers as a primary news source. Dr. Michael Griffin, professor of media studies at Macalester College and author of *Media and Community* says, "In the evolution of media platforms we have moved from choosing a program lineup on a particular broadcast network (ABC, CBS, NBC, or PBS) to 'surfing' cable TV, with many more channels competing to grab and hold our attention with increasingly overdramatized, politicized, and specifically targeted content, to the web, with an algorithmic, hyperlinked system designed to harvest clicks. The business activity we refer to as 'attention merchants' evolved from radio, television, and popular publications (e.g. 'the magazine stand') to the Web, which encourages an almost constant, addictive monitoring." Media platforms are now full participants in the attention economy, using sensationalism and opinion to attract and retain as many eyeballs as possible to deliver to advertisers.

Drawing Your Attention – and Keeping It

Clickbait is designed to draw a reader's attention to an article or video by using some form of sensationalized or perhaps even blatantly deceptive language. We have all seen them: "You won't believe how much money Kim Kardashian has under her mattress!" or "10 things about clickbait headlines that you always hate!" As Dr. Shyam Sundar, the James P. Jimirro Professor of Media Effects and co-director of the Media Effects Laboratory at the Bellisario College of Communications at Pennsylvania State University, says, "News outlets resort to hyping-up their stories by making them more sensational than they really are. Initially, clickbaits were used only by shady websites to get users to click through several pages in order to get more ad impressions. But now you see even respectable news outlets resorting to clickbaits in a desperate effort to not only attract readers but also to show good metrics of user engagement, which are important for earning advertising dollars."

Obviously, the downside of this approach is that it can disappoint readers who click and see that the content of the article does not match the headline. Furthermore, the inaccurate or sensationalized clickbait headline could impact the perception of the reader when it comes to the actual topic. A group of Australian researchers explored the effects of headlines that contained some element of misinformation. They found that misleading headlines or images can constrain elements of information processing and, perhaps more importantly, create a bias towards a specific interpretation of a news event. So if a headline reads, "There are a lot of questions about the honesty of President Abraham Lincoln," you might be inclined to click on it and discover that the content of the article is irrelevant to his honesty as a president (maybe the article described something silly like how several people have said that he once inflated his net worth to his wife, Mary Todd, when they were dating). You could read that article and understand the contents but still walk away from it thinking there are questions surrounding the honesty of Abraham Lincoln (hmm . . . and did he really deliver that Gettysburg Address?). Headlines designed to attract clicks through sensational language can bias the actual perceptions of the story even if the facts of the story do not match the sensationalism. It is one thing when the topic is frivolous, but it is another when the headline relates to real news that has real consequences.

The quality and reliability of information within the digital landscape today is filled with entities that have a number of political and commercial agendas that can create misinformation and take advantage of our biases. Griffin suggests that information becomes a currency of this digital environment, where the quality of information becomes secondary to its ability to become viral. In addition, sources work to develop content that is marketable to receptive and amenable audiences, leading to feedback loops and information silos. As he puts it, this environment expedites propaganda networks from both foreign and domestic players. Stories that do not have this sensationalist appeal, connecting with our political or moral sensibilities, will likely be secondary to what can cause the biggest splash. Opinion also replaces news, where media sources work to appeal to an audience segment providing either a biased take on headline news or predominantly opinion that will resonate with their audience. We see this in the divide of cable news channels with conservatives watching Fox News and liberals watching MSNBC. Digital media has similar outlets that appeal to our biases. During the weeks leading up to the 2020 election, competing cable news networks were not only providing biased perspectives on coverage of the election, but they were going as far as reporting completely different stories. It is difficult, if not impossible, to come to some degree of consensus as a country when we are not even working under the same set of facts.

There is clearly a blurred line when it comes to news and opinion. A 2019 Rand study conducted an analysis of broadcast television news, cable news, newspapers, and online journalism from 1989 to 2017. Using machine learning and text analysis, Rand examined content from the different platforms relative to "social attitude, sentiment, affect, subjectivity, and relation with authority." They found that content across all platforms continually moved towards more opinion, with 2000 being a critical year where cable news ratings began to rise. Instead of basic presentation of fact, broadcast news moved towards more conversation, opinion, and argument to match some of the content occurring on cable news. In 2018, Pew conducted a study of over 5,000 Americans, providing them with five statements that were factual and five statements that were opinion. Just 26% of the participants were able to identify the factual statements as factual and only 35% were able to label the opinion statements as opinion. Perhaps more importantly, they found that participants "were more likely to classify both factual and opinion statements as factual when they appealed most to their side."

Confirmation bias, a topic addressed in more detail later in this book, likely caused these individuals to think that the statements they agreed with were factual, whereas statements they disagreed with did not appear factual to them. Cable news channels appeal to that bias by confirming viewers' beliefs regarding any number of political and moral topics. Viewers tune in to receive validation of their beliefs. This becomes particularly worrisome when there is a blurred line between what is news and what is commentary. Many of these commentary programs look and act like news shows: an anchor sits behind a desk discussing current events just like the local 6 p.m. news. In essence, some cable news channels have a partnership with their viewers. Cable news gets the viewers' attention and ratings, and viewers get their positions confirmed. Repeating this daily process can create a polarized country. If anyone, regardless of party affiliation or perspective, has his or her views regularly confirmed regardless of validity, it creates a dogmatism that seems almost impossible to overcome. If someone tells me each and every day that I am correct about something, then I really believe I am correct!

Staying Informed

A 2019 Pew study indicates that 30–35% of Americans say they keep in-depth attention towards the news throughout the day. We engage push notifications on our smartphones, social media, and "breaking news" on television and radio throughout our day. In an age of instant gratification, we want the information and we want it now. News sources seize upon this desire and create as much breaking news as possible even if it isn't actually breaking news. In many cases, it can be several hours old or not worth the alarm that the media source is sounding.

Take a moment and think about your response when you are watching TV or listening to the radio and you hear the phrase "breaking news." What is your internal response? For many, it heightens attention. You likely think to yourself, "I better watch or listen because whatever is going to be shared might affect me right now." In fact, information, including breaking news, is a reward in and of itself, even if it may not affect you personally. Dopamine fuels that seeking behavior for new information. Researchers at the University of California scanned the brains of gamblers while they played a lottery game. They found that the anticipation of information, whether valuable to their winning or not, activated the same parts of the brain that are activated in the production of dopamine, which activates our seeking behaviors related to delicious foods and sex. You can see the implications of this study when it comes to our constant thirst for new information, specifically breaking news. We get a little shot of dopamine when there is the possibility of the novelty of breaking news or new information that might somehow impact our lives. Media sources seize upon this human aspect by constantly presenting and repackaging news and opinion as if it is new and breaking.

The notion of novelty when it comes to new information also impacts how it is shared across social media. Researchers at MIT examined 126,000 news stories over the course of an 11-year period. Using a variety of fact-checking groups, they were able to determine which of those stories were true and which were false. Controlling for bots (automated software that can tweet and retweet information), they were able to determine that false news spread much faster than real news. The false news consisted of topics from politics to urban legends to a host of other categories. Actually, false stories were 70% more likely to be retweeted than true stories, with true stories taking six times as long to have the same penetration as false news. As the researchers state, "When information is novel, it is not only surprising, but also more valuable, both from an information theoretic perspective in that it provides the greatest aid to decision-making, and from a social perspective in that it conveys social status on one that is 'in the know' or has access to unique 'inside' information." Being the first to share new information is important, whether it is a media conglomerate or individual retweeting on Twitter. We see the implications of the spread of this false news with the increased presence of conspiracy theories and unfounded narratives, each of which impact the country's political and social discourse.

How much do we actually engage with what we engage? According to Chartbeat, 55% of readers spend 15 seconds or less on a page. The average video watch time is 10 seconds. Obviously, these data reinforce the notion that we have short attention spans. However, it also causes us to question how informed we actually are regarding the news. As Sundar points out, "I think the public are more aware now than before of public figures and major events, but this awareness does not necessarily mean they are better informed. Since they are constantly drawn to eye candy coming at them from various directions, their attention is easily diverted. Therefore, they are less likely than previous generations to process the issues underlying the news stories in an effortful, let alone systematic, manner. And, even if they are willing to engage deeply with an issue, mainstream news media do not provide them that gratification." So there might be an element of awareness among the general public regarding the main issues and current events of the day, but the breadth of understanding of these issues may be limited. Media sources are tracking clicks and engagement time of viewers to encourage them to have more sensationalized content on the front ends of stories and videos to keep viewers engaged.

With the vast amount information that comes from various media sources, we actually have difficulty addressing all the information that is available to us. In 2018, 58% of Americans said that it was actually becoming more difficult to stay well-informed. That same survey from Gallup found that Americans are having increasing difficulty in sorting out facts relative to bias. Having a basic understanding of current issues without deep knowledge can also make us more susceptible to influences from social media. A similar Pew study in 2020 found that Americans who get their news primarily through social media tended to be less engaged and knowledgeable than individuals who got their news from other sources. Over the course of nine months, respondents were asked a series of 29 fact-based questions ranging from COVID-19 to economics to basic political questions. The group who got the least number of questions correct was those who relied upon social media for their news. Contrarily, those who followed social media for their news also tended to be more aware of unproven claims about COVID-19 or even conspiracy theories (such as individual people intentionally created COVID-19). It is important to note that the average age of these users skewed younger (with 48% of respondents between 18 and 29). However, it does highlight many of the elements of filter bubbles and confirmation bias that exist within social media, particularly if individuals are receiving their news via sharing from others. What are their friends and connections on social media saying when they are sharing this news? Similar to a clickbait headline, their statement while sharing the news could have a major impact on the perception of the reader even if the content of the story and the statement do not match. When it comes to social media, not only could the content of the story be biased, but the person delivering the biased story could also be biased!

We are drawn to bad news. Many, if not all of us, say that there is too much bad news in TV and print today, but we are still drawn to it. Researchers at McGill University asked participants to select news stories to read for what they thought was an eye-tracking study. They were told to select whichever stories they liked, positive or negative, and read them carefully for the purpose of the eye-tracking study. They found that participants were drawn to the negative news far more than the positive news, even though they said that they preferred positive news. Kalev Leetaru used sentiment mining, a technique that analyzes the nature of text, whether positive or negative, on *New York Times* articles between 1945 and 2005, as well as a variety of other news sources from 130 countries between 1979 and 2010. Outside of the influence of major news events, the tone of the stories progressively became more negative, beginning in the 1960s. Although there were a few periods, such as the 1980s, where the stories became a bit more positive, the overall trend over the past several decades has been towards events and even tone that highlights threats, suffering, and controversy. As Sundar says, "The saying goes, 'If it bleeds, it leads.' This has been a mantra for even traditional newspapers and local TV channels for several decades now."

The tiny part of the brain called the amygdala kicks into gear anytime we may sense danger. It is our warning signal when we might see a snake, a fire, or anything else that might be perceived as a threat. When the amygdala senses information that might indicate danger, it can increase heart rate and breathing, essentially activating hormones that prepare you to fight or flee. The amygdala is really important for our survival; think about centuries ago when we saw a wild animal approach us. The amygdala automatically activates our fight or flight response, triggered by emotions such as fear, anxiety, or anger. Regarding the news, the amygdala senses danger when it hears of bad news – even it that danger is far away, it draws our attention towards it. It can be difficult for that part of our brain to distinguish the difference between a real threat and one that is on a screen in front of us. Even though the rest of our body helps us rationalize, nevertheless the amygdala helps direct our attention towards bad news. Media sources take advantage of this by bringing more graphic videos, sensationalism, and breaking news (with that "doomish" music and the serious announcer voice: THIS IS BREAKING NEWS!).

Over time, regular exposure to negative news, and all of the sensationalism that accompanies it, gradually desensitizes viewers to the point of needing more and more outrageous, sensational, fear-evoking content to keep them engaged. This is an entertainment industry. In order to keep your attention, news outlets need to continue to push the envelope on our emotions to get a rise out of an increasingly numb consumer base. As we will discuss in a later chapter, this desensitizing of the viewer also has implications when it comes to compassion fatigue. Watching vivid images or hearing specific stories of horrific events on a daily basis that are sensationalized for the purpose of high viewership ratings can impact our ability to be compassionate towards victims of the events we regularly view. Whether explicitly or not, we can start to see bad events as normal or mundane, limiting our ability to respond to them in some tangible way.

There is also a natural tendency for us to take on a distorted view of the world via the news due to the availability heuristic. Psychologists Daniel Kahneman and Amos Tversky suggested that people estimate the probability of an event based upon how easily an instance of it comes to mind. That has particular implications for sensationalized news because stories that are particularly vivid or gruesome will obviously be remembered longer, making it more available in our minds and thus impacting our perception regarding the likelihood of it occurring again. In the 12 months following the September 11 terrorist attacks, many people opted to drive and not fly, even though statistically we all know that there are far fewer deaths from flying (40,000 a year driving in the U.S. compared to a few hundred on average flying). However, the images of the terrorist attacks or other plane crashes are front of mind for many, creating a bias and altering behavior in a potentially irrational way. Regular exposure to sensationalized, horrific events that are remembered for a long time due to their graphic nature can create this distorted view of the world.

Public distrust of the media is an ongoing issue. A 2019 Gallup poll found that 41% of Americans have a "great deal" or "fair amount" of trust in television, radio, and newspapers with regard to "fully, accurately, and fairly" reporting the news. Historically, that same poll, which dates back to 1972, found that 68% of Americans stated they trusted the media. Given the filter bubbles that exist within social media and even cable news, it stands to reason that there would be distrust of news outlets that are at least perceived to have some sort of bias that would prevent them from being a trusted news source. Illustrating some aspect of partisanship is a great way to attract loyal viewership. As Sundar says, "In the current political climate, news organizations have discovered that an easy way to evoke strong emotions and get more eyeballs is to stoke up partisan feelings. As a result, news sites and cable channels have become more extreme in their bias toward the left or right, resulting in great distrust of the media in general." Sensationalism, whether in the form of outrageous headlines designed to, well, invoke outrage, or clickbait designed to get more clicks on stories, also erodes public confidence in the media. In the short term, media outlets might get the viewers or clicks that they desire, but in the long term, these sensationalist practices can erode public trust.

Being Our Own News Editor

Steven Stosny, PhD, author of nine books and courses on healing and relationship repair, identifies four red flags as it relates to headline stress disorder: "First, you experience a raised pulse rate just before you check the news, and it increases the longer you're viewing or reading. Second, you think about news headlines repeatedly throughout the day and sometimes have trouble sleeping. Third, you're irritated with loved ones after the headlines. Finally, you only read or view articles that make you angry or resentful." There are lots of things we can do to address headline stress disorder. As Stosny says, "Aristotle pointed out that the only virtue is moderation. It's the ubiquity of headlines that does the damage. Limit exposure to a couple of times per day. Connect to your loved ones. Appreciate beauty in nature, arts, and crafts. Focus on what you can control, that is, your response. Focus on what you like and want more of, rather than what you don't like and don't want." It might even be just reminding yourself of the blessings or good things that are currently in your life, whether your family, your work, your health, or any other component of your life that you value, as well as realizing that the anxiety we are experiencing because of the news is not required. We do not have to subject ourselves to cable news or social media. Other peoples' hysteria or focus should not dictate where we direct our attention. Engaging in endless back and forth on social media or discussion boards is likely not going to solve anything. Focusing on the positive aspects of our lives, and engaging in them, can be far more valuable than stewing over the news.

We also have a great deal of power in addressing many of the challenges that come from the current news landscape. We can be cognizant of where we are getting our news, ensuring that we are relying upon trusted sources that are presenting an objective view of current events. As Griffin suggests, "A healthy consumption of news and information necessarily involves attention to multiple sources. But consuming multiple sources in and of itself will not necessarily help a person stay well-informed. And choosing sources based on one's perception of 'left-leaning' vs. 'right-leaning' is not helpful, in my opinion. The perceived political slant of a news source is not a good criterion on which to begin to plan a news diet. Instead, one should seek out news sources that have a reliable track record of responsible and transparent journalism." We should look at sensationalized headlines and clickbait with a critical eye to ensure that we have a full understanding of the story in spite of the hype. If our main objective is to be well-informed, we cannot passively trust one source to inform us of what is happening in our world. Media outlets are not designed to just inform us. They have a vested interest in attracting and retaining viewers.

This is not to suggest that all reporters and news organizations are terrible, biased people. Many of them have dedicated their life's work to informing the public. However, in order for us to be both well-informed and have a healthy relationship with the news, we have a responsibility to ourselves to question both the facts and the impact of those facts on ourselves and those around us. Griffin uses the analogy of a researcher choosing sources to conduct her research. The researcher doesn't look at the political affiliation of the source, but rather, the reputation, integrity, and quality of the source. It is no different in choosing a news source. Finding sources that have a proven track record for covering news and events in a transparent way will help ensure that we are well-informed regarding current events. We can limit our sources to only a small number and certainly monitor our consumption to avoid being overwhelmed with hyperbole and rhetoric. The rollercoaster that is the 24-hour news cycle is not a ride that we have to endure. We can pick good sources, limit push notifications, and be sensitive to the time we devote as well as to the anxiety we are feeling while still being well-informed.

CHAPTER 4

Instagram Worthy

"Years ago, every guy had just one picture of himself. Just one his entire life . . . [but] 50 years from now, it'll be, 'Hey. You want to see 100,000 pictures of my great-grandfather . . . and everything he did every day of his life?"

— Norm Macdonald

Growing up, when my family traveled on vacation, we would always take several disposable cameras. Unless we found a store while traveling, whatever number of shots that were in those cameras when we departed was what we had for the entire vacation. There was definitely rationing as we would put considerable thought into determining what was photo-worthy and what was not. There was no chance that we were going to spend any of our limited film on pictures of our dinner or selfies outside of the gas station. The cameras were meant for pictures of the highlights of the trip, memorializing our vacation to document for our memories and scrapbooks. Of course, after the vacation, the challenge was encouraging mom to take the film to be developed at the local drug store. Once developed, the pictures would usually sit on a coffee table for a few weeks, rarely to be viewed. Eventually, Grandma would take a look and ask all kinds of questions about where the photos were taken and why we took them. She sometimes would respond that she liked the photo, long before Facebook provided the same opportunity to like photos. I don't recall Grandma ever giving the "thumbs-up."

Cognitive offloading is the incorporation of some physical action to reduce cognitive demand, usually our memory. This practice has been around for as long as we have had the ability to write on stone and parchment or use cameras and phones to capture experiences. Given the limits of short-term memory, we can only actively hold a small amount of information at any one given time. With the rise of smartphones and virtual assistants, we have been able to transfer many of the items that we need to remember to our smartphones and not think twice about whether to remember them or not. This includes routes to get to different locations or reminders regarding scheduled meetings and trips to the dry cleaners. Once we start to rely on smartphones for memory, we tend to go back to them again and again. A team of researchers from UC Santa Cruz and the University of Illinois found that once participants were allowed to use their smartphone, specifically Google, to access facts during a trivia game, they repeatedly returned to Google for subsequent questions. The participants were divided into two groups: one team that could use their smartphones and one that could not. (I'm not sure I would want to be on the team that could not use smartphones. It doesn't seem like a fair fight.) The group that was allowed to use their smartphones tended to return to use it repeatedly, even if the subsequent questions were much easier. In fact, 30% of the group that previously used Google did not even attempt to answer the subsequent questions from memory; this group immediately referenced Google without even considering whether they knew the answer themselves. As lead author Benjamin Storm stated to *Science Daily*, "Our research shows that as we use the Internet to support and extend our memory we become more reliant on it. Whereas before, we might have tried to recall something on our own, now we don't bother. As more information becomes available via smartphones and other devices, we become progressively more reliant on it in our daily lives."

There is an element of cognitive offloading when we take pictures as well. Photos capture moments that we can relive for months and years after the event. We take photos with the objective of documenting the sights, sounds, and perhaps feelings of events for future reference. According to Infotrends, there were 1.2 trillion photos taken in 2017, with 200 million pictures uploaded to Facebook. We take pictures of everything, from each and every aspect of our vacations to the best grilled cheese sandwich ever to lots and lots of selfies. As Alixandra Barasch, assistant professor of marketing at the Stern School of Business at New York University, says, "People will give you a lot of reasons as to why we take photos for ourselves and document moments for the future (memory); share for social media because it is very basic (a human need) to connect with people. I want you to respond to my photo; to learn more about me; my identity; I want to show you that I am cool." We take and share photos to remember and perhaps more importantly, inform and impress others.

"Do You Remember Where This Was Taken?"

The act of taking pictures during an experience may also have a significant impact on our ability to remember that experience. Linda Henkel from Fairfield University asked a group of undergraduate students to take a tour of the university museum and take note of certain objects, either by observing or taking a picture of them. On the following day, she tested their memory of the objects. She found that participants were less able to recognize the objects that they photographed compared to the ones that they just visually observed. Henkel describes it as the photo-taking-impairment effect, where the individual relies upon technology to remember an experience rather than focusing their attention on it. The attentional resources used to take the photo, whether finding the right lighting, angle, and the act of using the device, and so on, could take away from what would otherwise be devoted to the actual object itself.

As we are using the cameras on our phones during important experiences, we could actually be losing at least a portion of the actual experience. We can go back to the photos or videos later to relive a component of the experience, but we may not be remembering the experience accurately because our attention was focused on the device rather than on the experience. There is a local park here in Washington that hosts a variety of youth sports camps. At every camp, there will be parents who use their smartphone to video record hours of footage of their child running up and down the soccer field (or sometimes just standing around with what appears to be little interest in being there). I always wonder if they will ever watch all of those hours of footage. Perhaps most importantly, I am curious whether the parent is capturing the actual experience with their memory. Sure they are fixated on their child and can see his or her face and movements throughout the experience, but what is it that the child is seeing during the experience? What is happening around the child or during the game? Our screens essentially become the boundaries of what we are experiencing. Most importantly from a cognitive perspective, given that the parent's attention is focused on their device, they are relying on it to capture their memory which may or may not be the same as if they were simply absorbed in the soccer camp, focusing their attention on both their child as well as the entire experience.

I Can't Wait to Post It!

The sharing of photos of our experiences on social media brings a new complexity to both our memories, as well as the nature of our actual experiences. Barasch and her colleagues conducted a series of experiments to explore the relationship between taking pictures for the purpose of sharing on social media and an individual's overall enjoyment of that experience. They found that individuals who take pictures for the sake of sharing tend to enjoy the experience less than if they were not sharing photos; curate photos of themselves smiling or posing rather than take more "candid" photos; and have increased anxiety over whether they are portrayed in the pictures in a positive light. When we take photos for the purpose of sharing, we tend to opt for a third-party perspective of the experience, where our focus shifts from experiencing the event to how it and the photos will be evaluated by others. As Barasch states, "When we are taking photos to share, our visual becomes more third-person and not first-person. It changes our lives in how we process events." When we share photos of experiences on social media with connections that we may not know, we are essentially inviting strangers who otherwise would not attend the event into our experience. Sometimes that is positive and sometimes it is not. As Barasch states, "By sharing photos, the goal is to invite others from social media into our experiences and incorporate those who were not in attendance, whether people we know or strangers." It seems as if every few weeks, one of my Facebook friends posts a picture of his or her grandparents sitting at the dinner table with the caption, "Dinner with the grandparents is so exciting!" More often than not, the look on the grandparents' faces sends the message of "Why are we taking a picture of dinner? We have had meatloaf for 50 years so why is this suddenly the Oscars?"

Sharing on social media alters the invite list for these experiences. Sometimes others who are part of those experiences are aware of this sharing and sometimes they are not, which is another topic as it relates to privacy and comfort. However, if our attentional resources are focused on the presentation of pictures on social media as opposed to the enjoyment of the experience, it will impact our immersion in that experience. There are a number of positive benefits that emanate from sharing on social media. People get to see different facets of our lives and learn more about who we are in a variety of contexts, from family gatherings to vacations to trips to the dentist. Like so many other aspects of our lives as they relate to technology and information, it is about our own goals that we are hoping to achieve. It could also be about thinking critically about who on social media we are sharing our photos with; strangers might be perfectly fine for pictures while in line to vote but "family only" might be better suited for reunions and other private events. With that thoughtful approach to who sees private events, we are more likely to record the actual event as it transpired, rather than curate it either by selectively posting only pictures that portray the event in a positive light or by actually altering the event for the purpose of positive pictures.

Not only can the sharing of photos on social media alter the nature of our experiences, it can also alter the experiences we even choose to engage in in the first place. If one of our primary motivations is to receive as many "likes" as possible on social media, then we may decide not to have dinner with the grandparents and do something more "Instagram worthy" instead. We might begin to consider future experiences from the lens of a content producer, perhaps at the expense of the enjoyment or utility of the experience. Some of us take that role as content producer seriously and some of us do not. For those who do, we might begin asking ourselves which experiences will gain the most traction on social media. Where should we go and what should we do that will gain this positive response? As Barasch states, "Sharing on social media shifts people's goals and motivations, including their choice of activities and experiences. Sharing makes us change our goals to undertake experiences more noteworthy. You're on vacation and choosing between activities; you will choose based upon what is the best sharing activity. You might go to the item that is 12th on the tourist list even if it is not something you want to do; you will go to something that is more shareable, which can outweigh your enjoyment of the experience." In essence, we are literally curating our lives for the sake of social media, rather than just curating the story of our lives as we discussed earlier. Each of us can only determine the authenticity of any of our life experiences, but it is hard to imagine that planning and experiencing our lives through the lens of maximizing social media attention is a path towards long-term fulfillment.

Given that so many people are posting pictures of vacations, dinners, new clothes, and the like, there can be this desire to "one-up" one another to gain the attention on social media that so many desire. Essentially, we can create an echo chamber of fabulous experiences on our social media feed – experiences that we may or may not have ever had! One-third of millennials stated that they purposely posted misleading pictures of their vacations, depicting an experience far better than it actually was. And 15% of Gen X and lesser numbers of Baby Boomers did the same. Their motivations for posting these misleading pictures was to make their followers envious and/or to compete with others who do the same. In some respect, it seems as if the act of capturing the moment has become more important than the actual moment itself. We spend so much time trying to find ways to depict that we are having the best vacation or the ideal family holiday that we are constantly thinking about what the next picture will be or, worse yet, trying to reconfigure the experience around finding the best picture to post on social media. If our primary objective is to capture the elements of a family reunion for the purpose of our own memories, we might take shots of each member of the family or candid shots when individuals may not be looking, depicting something that might really capture who they are (Aunt Debbie making her famous cookies or Uncle Doug once again fast asleep on the couch). In this approach, we are capturing the experience that we are having for the purpose of preserving it. Contrarily, if our focus is on how we present photos to others, it naturally will take away at least some of the focus from our experience of the actual event. It may not be a focus on what is actually happening, but what might be more compelling to another audience. We are, in some regard, inviting our social media audience into our experiences as we think about what would resonate with them. We might ask for certain poses that make things appear happier than they are or even wake up Uncle Doug to show him in the very best light.

We only have so much attention to devote to any given experience. If we are devoting attention towards the capturing of that experience, our ability to be fully immersed will be compromised. If we are taking pictures of an experience and posting those pictures on social media while the event is occurring, we are now placing additional demands on our attention and potentially compromising our ability to fully experience where we are and what we are doing. In this scenario, we are sacrificing a portion of our experience to jump back into the dopamine loop, where we constantly return to our phone to check to see how many likes the photos have received. Thus we are limiting our engagement with our experiences in two ways. First, we are altering our experience for the sake of pictures to post on social media, and second, we are detaching ourselves from the experience by focusing on our posting of the experience on social media . . . during the actual experience. As Barasch states, "The best thing to do is to isolate it from the experience. Having people freely document but try to leave the sharing process for after the fact. I tried it myself and it really helps a lot. Deferring it to later in the hotel room or whatever."

With all of the pictures and the many options that people have to share all of these experiences, one has to wonder how much people are actually looking at the photos we post in the first place. Sure, our photos and posts may receive numerous likes, but are people really looking at them in the way that we might think? With all of the information coming at us in this information age and the endless scrolling that occurs in social media, one has to wonder if all this trouble of altering our life experiences for the purpose of a few casual likes is really worth it. Selecting experiences solely for the purpose of producing fresh content for social media as opposed to things that we would love to do otherwise seems like an extreme sacrifice. I wonder if, after a year, we would make the same decisions. In other words, were the likes worth not doing what it was that we wanted to do in the first place? Were the likes worth altering our family reunions, vacations, and meals just so we can get more attention from friends, acquaintances, and strangers? Each of us has to answer that question for ourselves. It could be a valuable exercise now, looking back on your social media feed and reflecting upon those experiences. Did you alter some element of the experience just for social media? Did you spend a considerable amount of the experience thinking about how others would react to your depictions of that experience? Did it impact your enjoyment of that time? Taking pictures, even for the sake of our own memories, is a worthwhile endeavor. There is also nothing wrong with sharing our experiences with others. Perhaps we can balance our attention between immersion in the activity and photo-taking, allowing us the ability to see, listen, and feel all aspects of the event during times that we are not taking pictures. We can decide who should be on the "invite list" for these experiences by thoughtfully considering which connections on social media can have access to some of our photos. Like many things, there is a balance. We can find ways to live the experience that we are having while finding ways to document the experience separately. Taking a balanced and thoughtful approach to how and where we take photos and, perhaps more importantly, when and with whom we share them could help us place our enjoyment of our experiences as our highest priority. As trite as it sounds, we should first have the experience before attempting to share it with others.

CHAPTER 5

Who's the Pigeon Now?

As a kid, I had a beagle named Buffy. She was the nicest dog and served as a companion to a five-year-old who offered her little, if any, personal space. During our time together, I taught her a variety of tricks as I figured out pretty early on that I had the power, through all kinds of puppy snacks, to make her do things that she otherwise would not do. I taught her all of the standard tricks, including fetching different things and barking upon request. She would also go to bed on verbal command and shake hands upon request. With enough time and Italian sausages, I probably could have taught that dog to write a master's thesis! Humans are similar in many ways. Although not everyone writes a master's thesis (or is even willing to shake hands), we are all motivated by rewards of one form or another. They can be as basic as homeostatic (food and water) and reproductive (sex). Other rewards are intrinsic, meaning they are unconditioned and done for the pleasure of themselves. This could be taking a class for the pure enjoyment of learning, or playing basketball with a group of neighborhood kids. There is no tangible prize or payoff. You just do it for the joy of doing it. Extrinsic rewards are tangible and are usually conditioned, and more often than not they are related to money. We go to work and are motivated – sometimes primarily, sometimes entirely – by the money we receive in compensation for our time and effort. We can also be motivated by going to the gym to have better health and appearance to attract potential mates. We can be motivated by receiving a positive response from someone significant in our lives so we take out the trash or buy dinner or an expensive gift to receive that positive response. If the reward is positive and reinforced, we will continue to perform the action, particularly if it happens immediately after the action.

There is a reward pathway, known as the mesolimbic pathway, which facilitates our motivation for basic needs. Essentially, there are two experiences that we have with regard to rewards. The first phase is motivation, which encourages our seeking behaviors, consisting of all of the categories mentioned above. Our motivation is not only determined by outside stimuli, but also internal ones. Our seeking behavior is controlled by dopamine, a chemical produced in our brains that is key to motivating our behavior. Dopamine has taken on a sexy persona in pop culture as the "fun feeling" we experience when we eat delicious food, have sex, or engage in a positive social interaction. As a neurotransmitter, dopamine essentially acts as a messenger that travels among pathways in our brains between cells. Known as the "feel-good" transmitter, it regulates our attention, motivation, emotion, and learning. It is the expectation of the reward that is most powerful and influences our memory. So in essence, dopamine is important as it becomes active and motivates us when we expect to receive a reward. There is a desirable amount of dopamine that we all need. Drugs and alcohol can create a euphoric sensation by raising dopamine levels to a very high level, which can be quite unhealthy and lead to a number of health problems. On the contrary, if we have too little, we are not really motivated to do much of anything because we are less likely to be seeking pleasurable experiences. All in all, dopamine is a powerful tool in helping us seek, and eventually repeat, both vital and not-so-vital behaviors. The second component is the pleasure component, obviously valuable because without the reward, there is no seeking.

Burrhus Frederick (B.F.) Skinner, a psychology professor at Harvard, was one of the most influential psychologists of the last century. Although some of his work has been challenged over the past decades, Skinner articulated that free will was secondary to reward and punishment, basically known as operant conditioning. Through rewards and punishments, Skinner suggested that pigeons, rats, and ultimately humans could learn to do and repeat many behaviors. Through operant conditioning, subjects make a connection between a behavior and response, whether negative or positive. Using his famous Skinner box, he would place a hungry rat or a pigeon inside a controlled container, and over time the animal would begin to associate the pushing of a lever with receiving food. Rather than studying internal thoughts and motivation, Skinner placed an emphasis on what is observable, most notably behaviors in a given environment. So essentially, actions that are followed by a desirable outcome (reward) are likely to be repeated, whereas actions that are followed by an undesirable outcome (punishment) are likely to be avoided. For example, if your spouse or partner rewards you with a foot massage for starting a running regimen, you are more likely to continue to work out (assuming of course, that you enjoy foot massages). Conversely, if you are punished by your other half for eating cake after your doctor put you on a strict diet to lower your cholesterol, you may avoid the cake in the future (and maybe go running again to see if you can still receive that foot massage).

Incidentally, Skinner was also responsible for designing Project Pigeon, a program where pigeons would guide U.S. missiles onto enemy targets (yes, you read that correctly). Skinner trained pigeons to peck at an image of a target, usually an image of an enemy ship, by giving them food each time they successfully hit the image. Therefore, through operant conditioning, the pigeons repeatedly pecked at the target when presented with similar images. Once the training was completed, the pigeon would be placed in a sock inside an actual missile and as it was launched, the pigeon would naturally peck at the target (this time an actual target through a window and not an image) thinking it would receive food. Since the pigeons were wearing sensors, the pecking of the target would guide the missile towards the actual target. Although the U.S. Army funded, defunded, then re-funded the project, they ultimately could not get themselves to rely on pigeons as a defense weapon. It is important to note that in tests, the pigeons were remarkably successful in hitting the target, which shows the power of operant conditioning.

Keeping Us Pulling That Social Media Lever

Not only is the type of reward or punishment important in influencing behavior, but when the reward or punishment is presented is also important. If a reward is given for a fixed number of actions, this is known as a fixed-ratio reinforcement schedule. For example, a real estate agent will get a commission for each house she sells. Sell a house, get a reward (compensation). If you are hired to pick apples at an orchard, you might receive a certain amount of money after picking so many pounds or baskets of apples. You know that after completing so many actions, you will receive your reward. Contrarily, in a variable rewards schedule, the number of responses needed for a reward varies and is therefore unknown. The most common example here is slot machines. No one knows when a certain machine is going to pay out so people continue to play. People push the lever again and again, feeding it sums of money, in some cases despite mounting losses, not knowing when they will hit it big. In general, with a fixed set of actions or time, the reward is expected. They may stop their behavior after the reward, knowing they received what they were motivated to do. On the other hand, a varied reinforcement, whether in number of behaviors or time, can motivate the individual to continue a behavior as they are perpetually expecting a reward – which may or may not arrive (another reminder why casinos make so much money). Despite loss after loss, players continue to play, thinking that the next pull of the lever will be the payout.

Social media operates under a variable rewards schedule. As with the pigeons and rats in Skinner's box, we are also manipulated on social media by a variety of rewards at varying times. Like the rat that continues to press the lever to get the reward at different times, we continue to engage social media waiting for that varying reward to be granted to us. Similar to the gambler in the casino, we return to the table, in this case social media, thinking the next time will be the reward. Social media platforms and casinos are similar in that they determine the rules of the game and dispense enough rewards at sporadic times to keep us engaged. There are the two components of motivation and pleasure. Each time we receive some positive feedback, whether a like or positive comment, we receive that little shot of pleasure. Dopamine kicks in to continue to reinforce the motivation for us to post new content as well as check to see if there are new likes or comments. We begin a habit of engaging social media when we post content so that we can receive attention in the form of comments and likes. If we post something that receives an enormous amount of attention or likes, we are likely going to post it again. For example, if you take a picture of yourself at the top of a mountain and it received hundreds of likes, you are likely going to continue to post pictures like that in the future. If you really are enjoying all of the attention your picture is receiving, you might even visit your profile multiple times in a day or even in an hour, monitoring how many likes you have received. The timetable for receiving rewards varies, which again, like the slot machine in the casino, keeps you playing or in the case of social media, coming back again and again.

In his book *Hooked: How to Build Habit-Forming Products,* Nir Eyal, a Silicon Valley entrepreneur who founded several tech companies, describes how businesses and products can change behaviors and become part of an individual's habits. If you can make something part of a habit, then your frequency of use by the customer increases exponentially, which obviously leads to more revenue through purchases, site visits, and so on. The process starts with a trigger, which is essentially the cue that builds the habit. This could be an internal trigger, which is something that we want or need. As the name implies, an internal trigger is something that occurs within ourselves. For example, if we are feeling lonely, we visit Tinder or Facebook. An external trigger is what brings the user to the product or service. This could be a push notification letting us know that we received a comment on our Facebook post or a like on Instagram. An external trigger could also come from a gaming app challenging us to return to make it to the next level ("Can you beat the dragon and solve a math problem?"). The second phase is the action, which is the behavior that is anticipation of the reward. In this phase, think about dopamine fueling this seeking behavior. Designers develop the action to make it as easy as possible, making it "frictionless." It can be as simple as clicking the button on the push notification or, in terms of a slot machine, let's eliminate the lever altogether and just push a button to play again. (We will discuss the relationship between friction and habits later in the book.) The variable reward is the third phase, which for social media consists of new content or attention from others each time we log in. Finally, the investment is the action that improves the product in the future. If we find new content on Facebook and decide to repost it with a rant or a rave, we have now made an investment to continue the cycle going forward. We will want to return to Facebook to discover how people responded to what we reposted.

Chamath Palihapitiya is a significant voice in Silicon Valley. He started at AOL before joining Facebook during their biggest period of growth from 2005 to 2011. In his executive role there, he was charged with expanding the number of international users to the platform. On an evening in late 2017, speaking to a group of graduate students at Stanford, he was asked about his feeling in developing Facebook into what it is today and its impact on connections of people:

> *I feel tremendous guilt. I think we all knew in the back of our minds, even though we feigned this whole line, 'there probably aren't any bad consequences.' I think in the deep recesses of our minds we kind of knew something bad could happen, but I think the way we defined it was not like this. It literally is a point now where I think we've created tools that are ripping apart the social fabric of how society works. That is truly where we are. And I would encourage all of you, as the future leaders of the world, to really internalize how important this is. If you feed the beast, that beast will destroy you. If you push back on it, we have a chance to control it and rein it in. It is a point in time where people need a hard break from some of these tools and the things that you rely on. The short-term, dopamine-driven feedback loops that we've created are destroying how society works. No civil discourse, no cooperation, misinformation, mistruth, and it's not an American problem – this is not about Russian ads. This is a global problem. We're in a bad state of affairs right now, in my opinion. It is eroding the core foundations of how people behave. By and between each other. And I don't have a good solution. My solution is that I just don't use these tools anymore. It's created huge tension with my friends. Huge tensions in my social circles.*

We will discuss many of the implications of these dopamine-driven loops that he mentions in later chapters, but the genesis for much of this sustained engagement comes from the design of these platforms, using operant conditioning, providing rewards at unpredictable times that suck the user into returning again and again. Added to that element is the reward of attention, which on social media is the currency of likes and comments. That attention we seek becomes more difficult to achieve given that there are others on social media who are in the same competition with us, making it challenging to create posts that will compete for the limited attention of other users. This can lead to posts and pictures that can become more outrageous in an effort to gain more eyeballs and attention. All of this can lead to a number of behaviors and biases that we will discuss in later chapters. Think about the modern-day casino. It is designed as a predatory environment to encourage what Natasha Dow Schüll describes in her book *Addiction by Design* as "continuous gaming productivity," a term normally ascribed to factory workers. Here, consumers are making fewer decisions to cease their gambling, in particular their time playing slot machines. Special consideration has been taken to highlight both wins as well as small losses to encourage further gambling. The ceilings and carpet are designed to draw players into gaming as well as to maintain a cocoon-like feel to keep them gambling. The large levers are still on the slot machines, but now there are small buttons that your hand can rest on that will maximize the number of bets you can make within a short timeframe. The notion here eliminates the idea of choice and speeds up "production" for more bets. The variable rewards schedule also encourages further playing as the "next bet" is always the one that can bring the biggest reward. Creating an environment that eliminates decisions and makes players more comfortable keeps continuous gaming productive. Our smartphones, and particularly social media, are designed with these same predatory features to keep us engaged on the platform as much as possible.

Is the Reward Worth It?

So how do we extricate ourselves from the modern-day Skinner's box? First and foremost, we should reflect upon the reward we are actually receiving from social media and our smartphones to determine whether we are attaining what we need from an evolutionary perspective. We are seeking rewards that help keep us alive and stay connected and our phones are imitating those through artificial rewards, usually delayed, that keep us like the rats and pigeons pulling the lever in Skinner's box. Fred Muench, president of Partnership to End Addiction, suggests that we need to first reflect upon the value that social media is bringing to our lives. "Reflection is a powerful tool that can help you determine whether you're getting what you think you are getting from social media and your smartphone." As he describes it, you may find that you are getting a short-term reward through social media, such as attention in the form of likes and comments, but you need to determine whether all of that time and attention is really helping you with your long-term goals. That reflection can be as simple as a few minutes every morning removed from technology where you can focus on parts of your life that are giving you value and true rewards. "You have to examine your relationship with technology and where it's working and where it isn't. You can do that by delaying when you look at your phone first thing in the morning. When do you really need it?" During that reflection, you may also ask yourself if the time you are investing in social media is leading to more authentic interactions with others. If you use it as a springboard for connecting with others in person or even via phone or chat, then it may be a tool that leads to a more lasting reward. However, if social media in your life has evolved towards a social destination for you, then reflecting upon its value in your life could be worthwhile.

When it comes to social media and our relationship with our phones, we are the pigeons, impacted by the nature and frequency of rewards that may or may not have a positive long-term impact on our lives. Unlike those rats and pigeons, we have the opportunity to reflect upon the benefit of each of our experiences and determine whether or not we should invest more time and attention. As Muench puts it, "We are being manipulated via our smartphones and social media. We each need to determine if the reward is positively influencing our lives." That process of reflection can lead us to determine if the rewards are really worth the amount of time and attention that we are investing. Like the players on the slot machines, or even my little pal Buffy, sometimes the reward just isn't worth all the investment.

CHAPTER

A Habit of Distraction

You are outside working in the yard with your phone in your pocket and you receive a text message, which creates a push notification, which causes you to immediately take out your phone and read and respond to the message. After responding and following part of the usual "rabbit hole smartphone routine," you then open one of the social media apps and do a quick scroll, which causes you to watch a video of your aunt's cat, who apparently just learned how to play the violin. You have to comment and congratulate your aunt (and of course, the virtuoso feline). Meanwhile, nothing is getting done in the yard. You are standing there with the phone in your hand, next to the waiting lawnmower and an unkempt yard. What was supposed to take an hour took much longer because you were distracted multiple times by your smartphone and all of the apps that are constantly panhandling for your attention. What's worse is that the next time you plan to work in the yard, you will factor in the time it took you to complete the yard work, including your smartphone distractions and rabbit holes, only to determine that you do not have enough time for yard work that day.

Distraction is all around us. It comes from the screens, gadgets, humans, and a host of other living and nonliving entities that are around us at all of the time. Where are you reading this chapter? Are you on your couch at home or at a coffee shop? Is the television on with sound? What about your smartphone? Is it with you or in another room? If someone sends you a text message now, will you know it immediately? What about your thoughts? Is there anything that happened today that you have been thinking about that is particularly worrisome? Anything you're thinking about that is exciting you or making you anxious? While at work, 75% of us are distracted by technology, leading to procrastination and decreased focus, losing up to one full workday per week in addressing all the many sorts of digital notifications.

Our personal lives are only a bit better in this respect. Over 50% of respondents to a Pew Research study stated that their partner is often or sometimes distracted by their cell phones when they are trying to have a conversation with them. All of this distraction can lead to fewer creative ideas, decreased productivity, and missed opportunities for deeper relationships with those around us. Distraction, at its core, is something that takes our attention away from something else. A good measure to see how distracted you might be is to evaluate those to-do lists that you make for yourself at the beginning of a day or a week and see how many get checked off. Do you start with an ambitious list and regularly find yourself not completing all of the items on it? I often wonder if, over time, my to-do lists have become less and less ambitious because I am factoring in all of my distracted time. Regardless, we are all distracted and those distractions come from a variety of sources.

One of the most common sources is sensory distractions, which are external and consist of the sights and sounds that are happening around us. This can be everything from our smartphones to our noisy neighbor to the sounds that come from an open office plan. As we discussed earlier, our ability to filter many of these sights and sounds is dependent upon our ability to control our attention to focus on our task or conversation. We ignore a myriad of potential intrusions, from the weight of the glasses we might be wearing to the chair that is supporting us. How susceptible we are to distraction can be dependent upon a number of factors, including the complexity of a task. It takes cognitive resources to resist distractions, so if we are performing a difficult task, we may be focusing all of our resources on what we are doing and cannot afford distractions, such as a sound or sight. When parking his car in a tight parking spot, my friend Kostas will turn the radio off to focus on maneuvering the car into the space. Whether he is aware of it or not, he is freeing his attention from the sounds of the radio to his focus on driving. Given that attention is a zero-sum game, we have only so much of it, so altering our environment in order to focus on the most important task is wise. Working memory also plays a role in our susceptibility to be distracted. With more working memory, the less likely we are to be distracted by something outside of the task we are trying to perform. Also, we can be more apt to distraction if we are especially tired. A study of 234 people at Michigan State University found that people who were sleep deprived had a more difficult time completing basic tasks with external distractions than those who were not sleep deprived.

What Are You Thinking About?

We also have internal distractions, which are thoughts that tend to pull our attention away from whatever it is we might be focusing on. Our brains are wired for us to give preference to the things that are most important to us. So if we are upset or anxious about a fight that we had with our partner earlier in the day, it is likely going to be a source of emotional distraction for us throughout the day. Incidentally, internal distraction is actually far more prevalent than any external distraction. Matthew Killingsworth and Daniel Gilbert found that participants spend 47% of waking hours in some state of mind wandering. It did not even matter what the participants were doing or experiencing; their minds still wandered. Actually, the best predictor of their happiness was not even what they were experiencing, but what they were thinking. This is contrary to what we always assume, which is that we need to "do" something to make us happy. Think about that for a second. We spend enormous amounts of time and energy finding experiences, from vacations to spa days, to achieve some level of happiness. However, no matter where we go, happiness for many of us is dependent upon our state of mind. As Killingsworth and Gilbert state, "The human mind is a wandering mind. And a wandering mind is an unhappy mind. The ability to think about what is not happening is a cognitive achievement that comes at an emotional cost." We tend to emphasize the importance of doing what makes us happy, but in many regards, it is secondary to what is going on in our heads.

Sometimes even the presence of our devices creates distraction. Researchers at the University of Texas explored the impact of the presence of smartphones on individuals when performing a series of cognitive tasks. The 800 participants in the study were asked to place their smartphones either face down on their desk, in their pocket or bag, or in an entirely different room. They found that the group who had their smartphones placed in another room outperformed those who had the smartphones with them, even when the phones were silenced. The researchers suggest that the more noticeable the phone is to the individual, the more cognitive capacity it uses. Even that mental process of not thinking about it when present uses cognitive resources. Think about how often we put our phones face down in front of us during meetings or dinner, thinking we are essentially eliminating the distraction. Many of us like to place our smartphone face down on the seat next to us when we are driving, thinking that not seeing the screen will eliminate the distraction. In reality, even without the screen in full view, just the mere presence of the device steals some of our attentional resources that are likely better suited for our driving.

Our internal distraction is something that is merely a way of life for us. It is something that we continually do. Beverly Flaxington, expert in human behavior and author of *Self-Talk for a Calmer You*, suggests that these internal distractions are a dialogue that we perpetuate that takes us away from many aspects of our lives. "Mostly unknowingly we 'agree' to engage in self-talk that oftentimes distracts us and is self-defeating. Most people are not aware they are having conversations with themselves, and tearing their attention away from life itself. While they could be engaging in the moment, enjoying what's happening, solving a problem real-time, or practicing active listening – instead, they are having an internal dialogue about what might happen, what did happen, what they will do and when they will do it. Many times people are not living a real life, they are living the life inside their heads talking to themselves and never realizing they are doing it."

During the time that I have been writing this chapter, I became more sensitive to my own inner dialogue. I found that, more often than not, this self-talk was incredibly disruptive. Rather than focusing on a conversation with a friend, my mind would consider a myriad of potential topics that have almost nothing to do with that conversation or even my friend. By spending time ruminating over trivial things that happened in the past, it was taking away from my focus on this book or other projects. This self-talk that Flaxington refers to is different from reflection, where we are consciously examining our feelings or past experiences. When we are internally distracted through this inner dialogue, we are participating in a dialogue with ourselves that is taking away from our ability to be present.

We switch our attention every few minutes due to a distraction. If we are switching between more than one task at a time, we are multitasking. If we are writing a report at work and see a push notification for an email, we direct our attention to the content of the email while the report is still in front of us and nowhere close to being completed. As we discussed earlier, multitasking has its challenges. Adjusting our attention between multiple tasks makes for difficulty in storing information within our long-term memory. Think about talking on your cell phone while you are parking your car; it is very easy to forget where you parked because your attention was devoted towards your phone conversation. If I am on a voice call while walking into my gym locker room and drop off my things and go work out, I almost always have difficulty remembering which locker I selected to store my things because my attention was focused on my phone conversation and not the locker number of my stored items.

Media multitasking – using multiple devices at once – can also have an impact on our attention and memory. Researchers at Stanford University asked 80 subjects to complete a number of memory-related tasks while their brain activity was being monitored by an EEG. They found that those who were heavy media multitaskers tended to have more lapses in attention and difficulty remembering some of the images they were presented with. As Flaxington states, "The mind needs to be able to focus and we can only focus on one thing at a time. If you need to concentrate, many people think that breaking the monotony by reviewing a newsfeed, or reading Instagram posts or responding to a friend or even listening to music and singing along will help, but unfortunately these things tear your attention away from what you need to be doing."

There is an element of habit when we are talking about managing our distractions. Throughout our day, we habitually turn to our smartphones to scroll through social media or even just start a random text conversation with a friend or family member. When we are bored, we will turn to our smartphone while taking a break from work. Sometimes we even check our work email during off hours and weekends, not necessarily because we are expecting a priority item, but because we habitually just check it. Researchers at the University of Washington found four common triggers for smartphone use across all age groups. First, users turned to their smartphones when they had downtime, like when they were in line at a store or waiting for a friend. Second, they tended to turn to their smartphone before or during tedious and repetitive tasks. Third, people turned to smartphones during socially awkward situations. And finally, they looked to their smartphone when there was some anticipation of a message or notification. We invite these other tasks into what we are already doing, regularly causing disruptions to our personal and professional lives. Given the time it takes us to refocus, the cognitive resources and time that these distractions waste adds up quickly.

Breaking the Habit

In the book *Good Habits, Bad Habits*, Wendy Wood discusses the notion of habit and persistence. She references the famous Stanford study where preschool children were left in a room to see if they would eat a marshmallow placed in front of them. They were told that if they resisted, they would get two marshmallows. Once the marshmallow was placed in front of the child, the researcher left the room, and 75% of the children could not resist the marshmallow that was placed in front of them. This study has been referenced as a determinant of whether children have the persistence to hold off on short-term rewards for long-term gain. The lives of the children who participated in the study were followed to see how their self-control, or lack thereof, impacted their achievement. The researchers discovered that those who held out in eating the marshmallow tended to be more successful. This study suggested that those children who exhibit self-control at an early age would be more successful in many aspects of life going forward. Wood outlines a lesser-known component of that study where some children were able to last 10 minutes without eating the marshmallow when it was out of sight and only six minutes when it was in plain view. They were able to think about different things, sing songs, and so on, which helped distract them from staring at the marshmallow tempting them to consume it. As she suggests in her book, this highlights the power of situations in helping us with self-control. We can think about other things, as some of the children presented with the marshmallow did, or we can make the tempting item inaccessible to us so that we will not partake.

A Habit of Distraction

How we reconfigure our environment to deter temptation can be really powerful. We can designate specific times when we allow ourselves to be on social media or even available to text. If we have been dedicating an overwhelming amount of time to texting with friends, we can let them know that we are limiting our texting and will be engaging only during specific times. In general, we can work or study with our smartphones (powered off) in other rooms or in our bags or coats, eliminating the presence of the devices altogether. In his book *The Power of Habit,* Charles Duhigg outlines the habit loop, consisting of cue, habit, and reward. We receive some cue, which relative to technology is a push notification or a sound that informs us of something. The habit is to pick up the phone to check it and, of course, the reward consists of the dopamine hit that we receive from the like or comment or whatever it might be. By disrupting the cue, we can eliminate ourselves from this habit loop and take control over tasks that are draining our cognitive capacity.

We have the power to manage both our internal and external distractions. If we can simply identify the type and level of distraction that we are experiencing, we can make changes to help us be more focused and present. External distractions are relatively straightforward, as we create an environment that keeps us in the present, everything from the settings and location of our smartphone to the environment around us. We can develop agreements with members of our household to have "screen-free" time, which could be during dinner or first thing in the morning during a few moments of quiet and reflection. Distracted driving is a serious issue as people attempt to drive while texting or checking push notifications. We can put our phones in silent or airplane mode and, perhaps most importantly, make them less accessible to us throughout the day. Creating opportunities for friction in accessing our devices can be a powerful tool in breaking these habits. Like the children who created cognitive activities to distract themselves from the marshmallows, we can develop family activities during "screen-free" time or develop new habits like reading a book or exercising. With regard to internal distractions, we must first make a commitment to be present. As Flaxington suggests, "Awareness is the first step. Simply recognizing your thoughts are not in the present moment is an important milestone. Become aware of the 'voices' – what do they say? When might you be triggered to go into a full dialogue about something? It's helpful to bring yourself back to what's happening right NOW. If you can pull your attention back when you recognize the voices running rampant, that's a first big step." After taking these steps, it is important to reflect upon how the experience was different without the distraction, whether internal or external. How was it different? Did you learn something different about those closest to you because you weren't focused somehow on your device during the interaction? Did you feel freer from internal thoughts when you were consciously attempting to be present? Essentially, reflection can be an assessment of the ROI – the return on investment – of our time and attention. Taking a proactive approach to managing our environment, as well as the internal dialogue occurring within us, can go a long way in maximizing our focus on both our work and all of the other experiences that life has to offer. Each of us has to ask whether these habits, particularly those related to technology, are really paying dividends for us in our short- and long-term goals. Regardless, the process of examining them can be healthy no matter what you decide. Now that I have finished writing this chapter, I think I will go grab that phone in the other room.

CHAPTER 7

Tinder and I Are Registered at Amazon

Helen Morrison posted the first personal ad in the history of a newspaper in 1727 in the *Manchester Weekly Journal.* She proclaimed her desire for "a nice gentleman." It is unclear how her dating life evolved after posting such an ad, but it did get noticed. The mayor of Manchester had her placed into an insane asylum for four weeks upon reading the ad. That is perhaps the ultimate "swipe left." As time went on, newspapers regularly posted personal ads from those looking for romantic partners of one kind or another. In the 1970s, singles could meet via videocassette dating, where they would go to an office center and be interviewed on camera regarding their life's interests and goals. They would also watch the video recordings of potential matches to see who they might be interested in meeting. If there was a mutual interest, postcards would be sent via mail to both parties to potentially schedule a meeting. That process could take months with mailing back and forth before the first in-person connection. That is a long buildup to a first date! Historically, there has been a stigma attached to those who posted personal ads or participated in some sort of matchmaking because they were seen as not necessarily being able to attract a romantic partner on their own for some reason. As Moira Weigel, author of *Labor of Love: The Invention* *of Dating,* told *Atlas Obscura* in 2016, "A lot of articles in the late '80s and '90s would say, 'It's not just for losers anymore!' So you can tell everyone definitely thought it was for losers."

Fast forward to the present day: we are rarely using newspaper personals and certainly not videocassettes (please excuse the fast forward pun). The online dating industry made close to $3 billion in 2018. About 15% of all Americans have used or continue to use some sort of dating site or app. Tinder alone has 57 million users and 1.6 billion swipes per day. The numbers skew younger, with more adults under the age of 50 using it than those older. This likely could be because dating apps seem to be an extension of social media and the younger population has essentially grown up with the internet. We are also a busy society now, with individuals focused on their careers and in some cases moving from one region to another, making it difficult to find a suitable mate. Online dating brings us a large number of potential mates. We can swipe right or left on more people in a minute on Tinder than we can likely encounter in person in an entire week. We can also determine age preference, body type, and the like before even beginning the process on many of these dating apps, allowing us to look at profiles that fit our own preferences. Online dating can be very similar to shopping for a car online, where you can decide the make and model, and perhaps the "mileage" of potential mates. You can pick sporty or conservative, and even decide if you are looking for something more casual than long-term, which I guess relative to cars would be the distinction between buying and leasing.

Unlike meeting people in person, it is easier to have a sense of what people are looking for if they're on an online dating site. At the grocery store, that attractive guy in the produce section might be looking at you for any number of reasons . . . and he might be married. Online, that same guy could still be married, but at least you are not going to walk over to him and make a fool of yourself when his spouse or partner appears from behind the nectarines! Many people are also more comfortable striking up an online chat with someone rather than a conversation in person. If you are shy or introverted, you may not feel the same level of risk in messaging a person on an app that you would if you made the long walk from one end of the bar to the other to say hello to a stranger. Users of online dating sites also have a great deal of control over what other users (or potential mates) see when viewing their profile. When meeting a stranger in person, any number of someone's traits or behaviors could give that first impression. Online, you can carefully select the pictures you want to show as well as the language that describes yourself to potential mates. There are no "bad hair days" when it comes to online dating profiles. You may also use pictures or descriptions that you think will be more attractive to others, potentially bending the truth or just highlighting certain points over others. Through filtering and other means, we can alter the appearance of our own pictures to seem more attractive than we might naturally be.

You Look Just Like Your Profile Pictures . . . Kinda

Most online dating sites provide users the opportunity to describe themselves, including their hobbies and physical appearance as well as the chance to upload a limited number of photos. Almost all of the apps now offer users the chance to select age ranges, objective (what you are looking for, whether friends, relationships, or casual sex), and in some cases, height, weight, and race or ethnicity. You can search for other users on these apps within your geographic location or pick another city that you might be moving to or visiting. You might even be using one of the apps and find the person sitting next to you on the same app. (I know this for certain, because it has happened to me. I will share the details of that story in my next book!)

Pictures are worth a thousand words when it comes to online dating profiles. The color someone is wearing in the photos can even have an impact. Women tend to find pictures of men wearing red or with a red background more attractive than other colors. Jennifer Sedgewick and her colleagues at the University of Saskatchewan analyzed the selfies of men and women on Tinder and found that women tended to take pictures from above the waist and men tended to take them from below the waist. For men, taking the picture from below the waist made them appear taller whereas women took theirs above the waist to appear shorter. The authors suggest that these selfies are either intuitively taken from these angles or "consciously selected." All of this essentially means that people are putting a lot of time and thought into the precise selfie they post to attract a potential mate. As we discussed in previous chapters, we tend to post curated versions of ourselves on social media. Obviously, when it comes to online dating sites, curated versions of selfies might be an understatement. Self-presentation theory is essentially how we present ourselves to other people and our desire to control the impressions that other people might have about us. We all want people to have some impression about us, whether it is related to our co-workers thinking that we are smart or hardworking, or that current and potential mates find us attractive. With that in mind, if we are looking for a potential mate online, how we decide to present ourselves to potential matches is likely a big deal.

Sometimes the "best foot forward" that we are trying to present might not even be our actual foot! In a study of 1,000 individuals who participated in online dating, 53% said they lied in their profile, with women posting younger pictures of themselves and men lying about their jobs. Women and men also tend to post pictures of themselves as active people, showing that one time they went waterskiing to give the impression that they are active, even if they might spend their entire weekends on the couch snuggled up with Netflix and Häagen-Dazs.

Given the ease with which people can dismiss potential mates on these apps, there is an element of rejection in play as well. In a study of individuals who use Tinder, Jessica Strübel from the University of Rhode Island and Trent Petrie of the University of North Texas found that those who used Tinder reported less satisfaction with their bodies and overall appearance than those who did not use the app. As Strubel says, "They are comparing themselves, their appearance and their overall self-worth to each other." As a user on one of these dating apps, you are repeatedly subjected to an evaluation of what you think are the best components of yourself. If other users are not selecting your profile (and therefore you), you can begin to feel as if you are not attractive or interesting enough. In high school, I had to ask three different people to the prom, which meant that I was rejected twice. I candidly remember both of those rejections. (I'm not bitter; perhaps I'll send them both a copy of this book.) Now, with online dating, a user can be rejected twice within seconds! A study by the nonprofit group Center for Humane Technology in partnership with the app Moment, which tracks screen time, found that of the 200,000 people they surveyed, 77% of the users of Grindr, a popular gay dating/hookup app, were depressed. Perhaps all of that rejection, or at least the perception of rejection, can have a lasting impact on someone's feeling of self-worth. (Just as an aside, Candy Crush Saga was the app that made users the second-most unhappy at 71%, followed by Facebook in third place at 64%. On the flipside Calm,

Google Calendar, Headspace, and Insight Timer were all rated by the iPhone users who participated as happiest at 99%.)

There is an element of objectification that comes from looking at all these pictures, making a split-second decision whether the person is good-looking or interesting enough to warrant a swipe right or a hello (or worse yet, a "sup"). The regular exposure of both objectifying people as well as being objectified (and perhaps rejected) must have a lasting impact on current and future relationships. If, for example, we are being overly critical of someone for their height or weight online, how does that translate to the real people with whom we come into contact in our daily lives, especially when all of us are incapable of being seen through a filter like the photos on our phones. Researchers at the University of Connecticut examined the relationship between attractiveness and trustworthiness of online daters. Using enhanced and unenhanced photos, they found that men found attractive women to be less trustworthy, while women perceived attractive men to be more trustworthy. They speculate that men see the picture of the enhanced photo of the woman and suspect that the woman may have misrepresented her appearance in some way. Or, as it's called, "catfishing," where an online dating user creates a false online profile for one reason or another.

Choosing a Mate

As we will discuss in a later chapter, an inundation of choice makes us less likely to commit to one choice or, perhaps just as bad, makes us question the choices we have already made. Online dating offers a constant supply of more profiles with pretty pictures and captions that present the best self to others. The challenge, of course, is that it makes us more critical of the individual we might be meeting at any given time. What if that person has some imperfection (you know, like all humans)? A maximizer might be one who says to herself, "I want to check all of my options on Tinder to see if there is someone who does not have this same imperfection." As Linda and Charlie Bloom state, "Having a lot of options is attractive to us. More options and more choices is better. There is a downside to a lot of options. It gets very confusing. Resisting commitment because we know that making that decision we are automatically excluding an infinite number of possibilities. The myth is that you can have it all, but you can't have it all. They associate it with satisfaction with every aspect of their life and relationship."

The online dating apps are not different from other apps in the sense that they are designed to keep you logged into them for as long as possible. The idea of variable ratio reinforcement, where rewards are delivered to the user in unknown frequency, can have users returning to the app multiple times or for hours in one sitting. Users might find themselves not having any luck with attracting another user so they might stay on the app until they do. It is no different than playing the slot machines: Many feel that you have to play to win. It is just a matter of how much you are willing to invest and what you determine winning looks like. The large number of individuals who participate in online dating creates a massive number of potential options in finding a mate. It also creates choice overload, which can create significant issues when one is presented with multiple options.

Researchers at the University of Wisconsin-Madison explored the element of choice when it relates to overall happiness with a potential match from an online dating site. Similar to the jam study referenced in chapter 16 regarding choice, participants in this study who chose from a group of 24 potential matches were less satisfied with their choice than the participants who chose from only six options. One week later, some participants were allowed to change their selection. Those with the option to change their selection were less satisfied than those who did not have the option to make the change. As the authors suggest, "The more and high quality alternatives individuals believe they have, the less likely they will be satisfied with their romantic partner." It stands to reason that satisficers – those who make selections based upon their needs and preferences – would potentially be happier with their selection in a potential mate than a maximizer. Maximizers – those looking for the ideal and willing to explore all options – may find themselves endlessly meeting potential mates to find an ideal match, which as we know may never arrive. As the fable goes, a man searched the world for years and years, looking for the perfect woman. And then one day, he found her. Unfortunately, she was looking for the perfect man and it wasn't him.

With the large number of choices that online dating can provide us, some people find themselves scheduling multiple meetings with potential partners over the same week (or even the same evening!). Rather than engaging one person throughout the course of multiple conversations, some move right into the meeting phase to see if the attraction is real. As Dr. Kelly Campbell, professor of psychology at California State University, San Bernardino, says, "People should give a person a genuine shot before moving onto the next person. Rather than make three dates with different people in one day, just see one person over a period of time and see if anything develops. If not, ask what can be learned from the experience and whether anything should be changed for next time. For example, if you engaged in sex too soon, and the relationship ended, consider taking a more gradual approach next time." As with anything, when meeting people via an online dating app, we can learn from each experience to hopefully improve our chances of building something more long-term with a potential mate down the road.

As with social media, many of us look to online dating platforms as a barometer of our own self-worth, hoping for some element of validation from strangers on a website who only see a few posted pictures and a curated version of ourselves. As Strübel states, "People have to realize that their self-worth is internal, and it needs to come from people who are closest to them, whether their family or friends. Hoping for validation from strangers is a losing proposition." She points out that most users are aware that everyone is curating their very best self in their online profiles. However, there is still a sense of comparison, or in some cases lower self-esteem. It could be that users of online dating sites see the pictures of potential mates at the gym, petting kangaroos, or doing any other host of activities that might represent the very best of their lives and not necessarily buy into the fact that it is real but that they are not doing all of those activities themselves, which could lend itself to a case of FOMO.

Online dating sites can be helpful for many people to make new connections, whether friends or romantic interests. The real challenge is finding ways to use these tools to help us find whatever it is we are looking for, whether something long-term or short-term. If sites like Tinder, OKCupid, and Grindr are destinations in and of themselves, where we become overconsumed by the process and choice of selecting potential mates, we might struggle to find something meaningful and long-term. However, each user brings their own objectives to these sites. Recognition of some of the challenges and pitfalls of these sites can be helpful not only in finding good connections, but also in limiting both the anguish and the choice overload that can come from these platforms. Dating apps, like trips to the shopping mall, are most useful if we know what we want, what we are willing to spend, and of course, the return policy.

CHAPTER

Confirmation Bias

"What the human being is best at doing is interpreting all new information so that their prior conclusions remain intact."

— Warren Buffett

From where do your political and social perspectives emanate? When you think about your journey in being liberal, conservative, moderate, and so on, where exactly did it all begin? Not a question that you want to ask at a cocktail party, but interesting when you consider each of our journeys relative to what we hold as true and perhaps right. Within our political positions, moral and religious beliefs, and stances on social issues, we have had at least the opportunity to hear a conflicting argument or data regarding our position. Perhaps we are ignoring conflicting arguments from other perspectives because we have limited our information consumption entirely to sources that are consistent with our positions. Maybe we even eliminated contact with friends and family who have conflicting views, or perhaps unfriended those on social media who see it from a different perspective. Many of us develop a position and then seek out information that confirms that belief and ignore data or facts that might refute our position. We might even remember instances where that position was supported and not remember instances where our position was refuted, even if we were exposing ourselves to objective reporting and information. This trajectory – from taking a position, seeking information that supports it at the expense of information that refutes it, clinging to sources that will support our position, and even to remembering instances that support our position – is confirmation bias.

Confirmation bias is a tendency to interpret ideas and situations according to an existing set of our own beliefs or experiences. We have a specific idea regarding a topic and hold to that belief at the expense of contrary information and, in some cases, opt not to even search for contrary information. As Nobel Prize–winning psychologist Daniel Kahneman says, "Confirmation bias comes from when you have an interpretation, and you adopt it, and then, top down, you force everything to fit that interpretation." For example, your first impression is that Deidre is a poor employee. Maybe it was the initial meeting that you had with her where she was having a bad day or maybe you spoke with someone in the office who had a personal issue with her and gave you a bad impression of Deidre. Based upon that initial information (and perhaps subsequent bias), you then only search for evidence of her weaknesses and ignore evidence about her positive work performance. So essentially, any hypothesis that you develop about Deidre can succeed with some information "cherry-picking." To the contrary, if your initial impression is that Deidre is a great employee, you could then find yourself searching for evidence that supports that claim as well and perhaps ignore any poor reviews or negative information about Deidre. You might even say that the visible project that she led that was delivered late and way over budget was not her fault (regardless of whether it was or not). Confirmation bias also exists in the way we remember information, as we tend to hold onto data that supports our position or preexisting belief. With Deidre, you might fail even to remember that there were serious issues with the project she managed. It is an element of selective recall, just as we only recall all of the wonderful things that we said to our in-laws last Thanksgiving as opposed to the things we said that were not as pleasant. Contrary to that position, our spouse or partner might have the preexisting belief that we are not friendly to his or her side of the family and only remember the things we said that weren't as agreeable. Our worldview can shape how we collect, value, and even remember information, sometimes with significant implications.

I Knew It the Whole Time!

In a study from Germany of 75 psychiatrists and 75 medical students, 13% of the psychiatrists and 25% of the medical students showed confirmation bias after a preliminary patient diagnosis. The psychiatrists and medical students were far more likely to search for evidence that confirmed their preliminary diagnosis than to search for information that countered it. For those individuals, their preliminary diagnosis did not just sway their final diagnosis; it may have actually influenced the process by which they sought information even to arrive at the final prognosis! Falling into the trap of making an initial diagnosis and then searching only for evidence that confirms it can be easy to do, especially if someone is working in a situation where time is of the essence. Think about any potential preliminary diagnoses we have when it comes to a variety of work and social situations. We make instant judgments and then filter data to confirm that judgment, closing us off to contradictory evidence that could challenge our assumptions, in many cases at our own expense. We see this with people we meet, experiences, and all types of work situations where initial impressions not only instantly create a narrative, but also impact how we filter any additional information that we might receive.

Emotionally charged issues tend to lend themselves to confirmation bias. Issues such as gun control, abortion, and climate change all are very sensitive for individuals on both sides of the argument. Thinking objectively, it is not too difficult to remember instances in the news where many of those emotionally charged topics have data to support both sides of the argument (more guns would lead to a safer society – and more guns would lead to the loss of more human life). In some cases, topics that tend to be more complicated or nuanced lend themselves to confirmation bias, because no definitive or clear "truth" suddenly appears. Climate change is one of those topics. It seems as if every time we have a record high or low temperature, those on both sides of the issue discuss how it is and is not happening, citing data that confirms their position. A group of researchers at Stanford studied two groups of students, one group in support of capital punishment as a deterrent to crime and the other opposed to it. Each group was asked to respond to two equally compelling yet fake stories regarding the efficacy of capital punishment as a crime deterrent. Both groups rated the studies that confirmed their beliefs higher than the study that challenged their beliefs. At the end of the study, the participants were once again asked about their beliefs and both groups, regardless of stance, became even more entrenched. Even when exposed to data that challenges our preexisting position, we can dismiss it entirely and instead focus on that which supports our position.

It seems as if whatever our position, we can find a news source that will cater to it. Thinking about the economics of information, where more eyeballs means more revenue, news sources like MSNBC and Fox News find their niche and attract individuals who tend to have a similar perspective. Within social media platforms, user time on their sites means more revenue. Therefore, there is an objective to expose the user to news and information that confirms their positions. We feel better when our beliefs are confirmed. Algorithms designed to give us information that confirms our beliefs are prevalent on Facebook and Twitter. If all of our Facebook friends are roughly the same race and sexual orientation, and share similar experiences and backgrounds, we will likely have a homogenous perspective on certain events. As mentioned earlier, there are great benefits to being part of a group with this shared sense of belonging. Where it becomes an issue is when these homogenous groups create echo chambers that dismiss or become hostile to any information (or individual identities) contrary to the beliefs of the group.

Echo chambers can also be breeding grounds for radicalization as individuals' statements regarding given topics within these groups are constantly supported. People who communicate only with people who agree with them become more confident in their beliefs. Essentially, your perspective on a given topic is flawless because everyone you spoke with about it says they agree with you. Essentially, "everyone is saying it and sees it the same way as I do," when in reality, everyone with whom you come into contact sees it that way because you have cut off all other perspectives and information sources. Individuals who move towards the fringe in their beliefs can create further polarization and limit discourse, which benefits no one.

The expression "birds of a feather flock together" existed long before the invention of social media. Aristotle stated that individuals "love those who are like themselves." Historically, people of like mind and experiences tend to share a common bond. This could be related to socioeconomic status, age, gender, race, religion, sexual orientation, or a myriad of other traits, experiences, or identities.

We value those who see the world in a similar way to us. The term "homophily" describes our desire to seek out individuals who are similar to us. Our connection to those online is no different. We have seen the presence of homophily in social media sites, including our Facebook friends, Twitter connections, and the like. There can be great power in sharing similar experiences and a common bond with those like us who are not geographically close. We can feel accepted by others who understand our journey, or we can find a space to discuss some of the challenges that we all face and how to overcome them. This can be especially true for individuals who feel left out within social circles in their community for some reason, or perhaps do not have a community at all. Of course, the downside of these homogenous groups is that it can create an echo chamber where our ideas and positions are merely reinforced by those with a similar perspective. There are no opportunities for ideas to be challenged by those with differing opinions.

Sources That Support Our Biases

Several years ago, the *Wall Street Journal* published a series called "Blue Feed, Red Feed." This project was designed to showcase social media content relative to a variety of topics. In order to be listed, news articles had to be shared 100 times or more by Facebook users who self-described themselves as very liberal, liberal, neutral, conservative, or very conservative. Facebook tracked and analyzed this content for six months of 10.1 million of its users. You can select any number of topics from President Trump to guns and abortion. When you select guns, the blue feed has headlines that discuss how a Republican congresswoman is peppered with questions and boos at a town hall, while the red feed news sources tout how the Dems are pushing for gun control after a police mass shooting. The subject, language, and even the statistics are designed to elicit an emotional response from the reader even though the reader has a dramatically different perspective. Living in an information age where quantities of news are in large supply but quality may encompass a large spectrum, from reputable to not-so-reputable sources, we each have the ability to search for information, credible or not, that supports our position. We can select from the menu of information sources available to us in the same way we select movies on Netflix: more of a comedy person, here is a list of top comedies; more liberal leaning, here is a list of liberal-leaning news sources. Rather than the information we receive creating our positions and opinions on current events, the positions we have on current events are shaping the information sources we select. In this sense, we are not being informed as much as we are being reinforced.

YouTube has over 1.5 billion subscribers who visit the site for close to a billion hours of screen time per day. This screen time consists of a variety of recorded content, from old television shows to homemade videos, infomercials, and quite frankly, a topic focused on just about anything you can imagine. YouTube uses algorithms to recommend other videos for the user to view based upon previously viewed videos. As of 2018, up to 70% of the videos that individuals view on YouTube are from these algorithms. This approach forces users into what is called "filter bubbles" where sites develop a playlist of content that they suspect you want to view given your past videos. Through YouTube, Google searches, and other social media including our Facebook newsfeeds, we become isolated into our filter bubbles, hearing only perspectives that support our existing positions. As discussed in previous chapters, the incentive for sites to create these filter bubbles is to give users what they want, which increases user screen time, which leads to more advertising dollars. I just visited YouTube and typed "UFOs are real" and I was able to watch "U.S. Navy confirms UFO videos are the real deal," followed by "Declassified UFO videos," followed by a myriad of other videos about the presence of UFOs. I then typed in "UFOs are fake" and found "the best fake UFO videos" followed by videos such as "Top 5 UFO video hoax tips" and a host of other similar videos. Although there were pro-UFO video suggestions in both searches, it is clear that if I really want to find videos that confirm that UFOs do or do not exist, I can find them on YouTube. This occurs during millions of searches per day with many topics far more important than UFOs.

Imagine if you spend three to four hours per day living in these filter bubbles and echo chambers on Facebook, Twitter, or YouTube. Each day you are watching and reading news that confirms your belief about any given topic. How in the world will you be reasonably able to participate in a respectful discourse about that topic with someone who has another viewpoint or a different life experience? What about those who are on the same site for three to four hours in a filter bubble with an opposing point of view? Filter bubbles and echo chambers are the equivalent of a "yes man" who follows you around all day telling you how correct you might be about a given topic. That "yes man" feeds you new information and data that reminds you that you are correct. With this manner in which we consume news and information, it is no wonder that we are so polarized. The natural push and pull of a democracy, an organization, or even a household is inherently a good thing. Hearing differing viewpoints regarding the same subject matter is beneficial. Every time someone has a serious medical condition and speaks with a physician, one of the first responses from loved ones is commonly "let's get a second opinion." Even if we are thrilled that the diagnosis is what we had hoped, the implications of an incorrect medical evaluation are significant. When I was having issues with my car, I would always get a cost estimate from the local mechanic and then call a friend who knew cars to ask, "Does this sound right?" A process where there are multiple (and hopefully objective) data sources is a good thing, particularly regarding topics that are complicated and important.

Countering the effects of confirmation bias, echo chambers, and filter bubbles is no small order. However, there are steps that each of us can take to limit the power of these polarizing mechanisms. A simple yet powerful first step is merely acknowledging that confirmation bias exists in all of us. We can recognize that we might not be visiting sites or engaging individuals who provide contrary evidence to our worldview. If we constantly ask ourselves whether we are hearing both sides of a discussion (rather than argument), it can benefit all of us. It is not necessarily a matter of changing our beliefs or admitting that we are wrong (although we might be). Rather, it is having a full understanding of an issue and objectively evaluating the data to determine a position. In some cases, the task of countering confirmation bias might be even more daunting, as individuals do not even want to have a balanced perspective on some issues.

As with the students in the Stanford study regarding capital punishment, exposure to data and research from multiple perspectives is not a quick fix to address these biases. However, we can each make a commitment to objectively engaging the other sides of issues maybe not to change our minds but at least to hear the other side's perspective. Making a commitment to engage others in respectful dialogue about topics can go a long way not only towards hearing others' perspective, but perhaps make Thanksgiving dinner with the family a little more pleasant. Is it really necessary to unfriend our friends and family on social media over political issues? I am not dismissing the passion and importance of these matters, but isolating ourselves without engaging others and, more importantly, differing perspectives is not going to advance our dialogue. It does not mean that we have to agree on everything, but if we can even articulate the other side's argument, we can have a better sense of where they are coming from and see others not as "the other side" but as equally important humans who just have a different perspective that may or may be informed by a different life journey.

Emotional self-control can also be a powerful tool. Similar to engaging many other forms of technology, we should constantly be recognizing and monitoring our own feelings while obtaining information regarding a specific topic. For example, Sheila could have a very dogmatic view regarding gun control. When hearing new information regarding gun-related violence or data regarding past incidents, Sheila could be self-aware about her own emotional reactions to this information. In this case, I am not suggesting Sheila is wrong (no one knows because I purposely didn't share her position), but she (and all of us) have a better chance of having a full understanding of a topic if we are calmly evaluating all of the news and information to which we are being exposed. Sheila might even actively look for evidence that refutes her position, helping her actually feel better about taking the right position. It is also not a matter of being less passionate about our beliefs in the least bit. Sheila may have had a very serious life event that has informed her worldview regarding gun control. Through her experiences, she could feel empowered in some way to get involved and volunteer to help others. However, if we desire objectivity and ultimately discourse that leads to positive change for everyone, we would all be well-served by monitoring our own emotions so we are objectively evaluating information and source. If the news happens to be from a discredited source, then our objectivity and our willingness to move out of our echo chambers will help us make the correct determination.

Empathy can perhaps be the most powerful tool in eliminating confirmation bias. Seeing the perspective of other human beings, particularly if there is pain and suffering, can help us be more open to opposing points of view. Whether they are Facebook profiles, Instagram pictures, or topics of news stories or policy decisions, they are all representative of actual human beings. They may or may not be part of our own echo chamber and we may not have many or even any shared experiences, but remembering the human element will serve us well in being rational, objective, and respectful as we engage news and information, and most importantly each other, both online and in person. As voters and participants in this democracy, we have a vested interest in being well-informed and objective in making decisions that will impact both our personal best interests as well as those of our communities and nation. We might "win the battle" if we stay inside our echo chambers, but we could lose the war if we are not searching for and celebrating the truth – whether we like it or not.

CHAPTER

Compassion Fatigue

Cole started his career as a resident physician in Atlanta in the mid-1980s. During that period, an increasing number of patients were diagnosed and treated for what had recently been identified as HIV/AIDS. It was a period when a diagnosis almost certainly meant death. As a resident physician, Cole began to see firsthand how many of these patients were treated while in the hospital. As Cole describes it, "When AIDS patients were in ICU rooms, meal service workers would shove their meals under the door and push the tray with a broomstick into the middle of their room. They did not want to be close to these patients. Nurses were terrified. Everyone was terrified." This fear of the unknown led to poor treatment of these patients, particularly those who were gay and, in many cases, alienated from their families during the last and very painful ends of their lives. It was during that time and witnessing the suffering of these patients that Cole realized that he wanted to devote his professional career to helping AIDS patients.

During the first 10 years of his career, there was no known cure or even much of a treatment for HIV/AIDS. "My role was to try to make their remaining days as comfortable as possible." Cole worked to comfort these patients as best as he could, listening to their fears and concerns in the absence of family and friends. "Some doctors were known as 'skateboard doctors' that would fly in and out. They would see 10–12 patients an hour. I wanted to listen to each patient so I might see only four or so per hour. . . . One day I saw a patient in the ICU alone and crying. I walked in and just held his hand as he died . . . I would hug every patient. They were part of the family. They would bring their partners, friends, and in some cases parents to my office. Everyone on the staff all wanted to be there. And they were the warmest people that I ever met." Throughout this time and without effective treatment, Cole was guided by compassion in helping these patients through the most difficult and final days of their lives.

Years passed without a cure but with an abundance of new patients. Cole decided to try to protect himself emotionally from the impact of treating these terminally ill patients. "I reached a point where I could not attend anymore memorial services. It was just too hard. I could not take it anymore. I had to protect myself from the pain," he said. "I can remember a nurse who I worked with coming to me and crying one day saying, 'I just can't do this anymore. It's too much.' She found another job in healthcare that was not as emotionally taxing. We helped these people as best as we could, but it took an emotional and physical toll on all of us."

Compassion fatigue is a state of emotional and physical exhaustion from repeated exposure to some element of human need or suffering. The term, sometimes also referred to as the negative cost of caring, is usually associated with first responders, therapists, and healthcare workers who are in regular contact with people during extraordinarily difficult periods in their lives. In many cases, the very trait of compassion that attracts a professional to a helping career can erode, particularly if they are unable to exercise self-care both physically and emotionally. Individuals who are primary caregivers can also experience compassion fatigue as they are constantly helping someone, perhaps a loved one, who has an intense and constant need for care. Journalists who are regularly on the scene to cover tragedy can become desensitized to the realities that they are reporting. Symptoms can include anxiety, exhaustion, sleep disorders, and emotional disconnection. In the case of Cole, he was constantly treating people who were experiencing intense suffering, and unfortunately had limited tools to help alleviate the cause of their suffering. The response to human suffering can take an emotional toll on the ones who raise their hands to help.

Playing to Our Empathetic Side

We are hardwired to be empathetic. As Charles Figley, a pioneer in the area of research on compassion fatigue, states, "We are born with compassion. It is part of the human condition. Understanding the world from another person's perspective is critical to our collective survival." Having a sense of life "in other people's shoes" is critical in order to help those who are suffering, as well as to address issues of social and economic disparity. If we have no sense of the lived experience of other people, we are living life as if the only worldview is ours. "I am doing fine so everyone else must be as well." At the same time, if everyone lacks empathy, we may have difficulty getting help when we need it as well. Professionals like Cole can experience compassion fatigue when there is still a strong desire to help, but they feel powerless to help, either because they do not have the tools or because the need is overwhelming. As Figley states, "compassion fatigue becomes an issue when our abilities to help are low yet our expectations regarding the outcome are high."

If empathetic professionals like Cole can experience compassion fatigue due to regular access to human suffering, it stands to reason that so too can the average consumer of news and information. The news cycle is dominated by threats of war, violence, natural disasters, and all kinds of human suffering. We see the human toll of violence and the aftermath of those lost to crime and disaster. Every day brings bad news, or at a minimum a threat of some sort, which is dissected in endless detail on cable news and social media. The availability of video content from a myriad of sources means we are even more accessible to graphic news from anywhere in the world. As we all know, there are very few news stories where the reporter on the street says, "All is well here. Everyone is happy and healthy. Back to you in the studio." By its very nature, news in many regards is bad.

As discussed in previous chapters, the push for attention from information sources of all kinds drives more graphic video. Many sources advertise that their coverage means you as the viewer "are there." It is no longer enough to discuss the plane crash verbally. Instead, we see video footage of the wreckage and perhaps even watch rescue workers take bodies away from the debris. We see the graphic videos of the effects of violence and natural disasters up close. We see the faces of the victims, and in many cases the grief of the families. In most cases, these videos are showing people – some near, some far – at the most difficult moment of their entire lives. Given the ease of video transmission, we sometimes see raw footage, unedited but shown to get the story out there first. In a 30-minute period, we bounce around to multiple human tragedies, with each receiving their five minutes of "bad news fame." Sensationalism brings with it vivid details of human suffering that hold our attention and keep us watching. Even from the vantage point of our couch, our hardwired empathy is affected on some level. With all of the human suffering and tragedy we see on our screens, the news cannot possibly be merely a factual experience. It is an emotional one that, over time, takes a toll.

Over half of Americans surveyed by the American Psychological Association say the news causes them stress. The repeated images of human and natural tragedies can cause as much stress via TV or social media as if you were actually at the event yourself. In a 2014 survey, researchers from UC Irvine found that individuals watching repeated videos of the Boston Marathon bombing on the news experienced more stress than those who were actually there when it happened. As Figley writes, "We have not been directly exposed to the trauma scene, but we hear the story told with such intensity, or we hear similar stories so often, or we have the gift and curse of extreme empathy and we suffer. We feel the feelings of our clients. We experience their fears. We dream their dreams. Eventually, we lose a certain spark of optimism, humor, and hope. We tire. We aren't sick, but we aren't ourselves."

Back in the 1990s, Katherine Kinnick and her colleagues explored the presence of compassion fatigue as it relates to a number of social problems. They found that mass media contributed to compassion fatigue in two ways. First, viewers develop compassion fatigue through constant exposure to videos and images that viewers find difficult to view, creating avoidance. Second, there was a desensitization regarding several of the topics as viewers were exposed to repeated and negative stimuli. They also found that presenting social problems without a clear solution led to compassion fatigue. The media contributes to compassion fatigue by emphasizing the sensational, repeated bad news, examining the underlying problems with a lack of context, and presenting problems that do not have stated solutions. Over time, the constant exposure to the suffering of others without a clear path to assist can make one numb to the plight of others. In 2020, Facebook reached a $52 million settlement with current and former content moderators to compensate them for many of the mental health issues that they encountered through moderation of violence, rape, animal abuse, and other images of brutality that the moderators were responsible for viewing and ultimately removing. Many of the moderators stated that the images haunted them in their sleep and may have even contributed to PTSD – certainly a human response to the repeated exposure of the suffering of others.

The Power of Compassion

There can also be tremendous power in the media illustrating the plight of others to prompt action. In 2015, a photo of three-year-old Alan Kurdi lying facedown on a beach in Turkey captured the attention of the world. The boy's lifeless body washed ashore after his family's boat carrying a group of Syrian refugees capsized as they were trying to reach Europe. Up until that time, the humanitarian crisis in Syria was not on the public's radar. Alan's photo grabbed the attention of the world, eliciting donations to the Swedish Red Cross 55 times greater in the week following the photograph than before. The plight of the Syrian refugee became part of the international conversation, with governments around the world discussing ways to help. When people saw Alan's little lifeless body on the shore, the humanitarian crisis became very real. Considering that the picture showed Alan's body facedown, some likely imagined him to have a face similar to a child in their own lives, making it even more powerful. Perhaps the image of a lifeless child was beyond our normal diet of sensational and graphic videos and jarred us into action. In a paper that analyzed the world's response to the picture, Paul Slovic and his colleagues stated, "Alan woke the world briefly, providing a window of opportunity during which people and their governments began paying attention to the Syrian refugee crisis." There are tangible benefits to hearing the story of human suffering if we can find ways both to manage how much of it we are exposed to as well as monitor our response to it all.

It is important that we are educated voters, knowing relevant issues that affect both our neighbors and ourselves. Whether we are conservative or liberal, it is in all of our best interests to hold elected officials accountable to the communities they serve. Having a sense of the news, and the plight of those who are suffering near and far, enables us to find ways to make the world a better place. With that said, we can manage the amount of news and information that we are exposed to on a daily basis. It is not healthy for us to sit for five hours to watch repeated videos, commentary, and opinion about violence, scandals, and natural disasters. We can self-monitor our own internal reactions to the news. We can make thoughtful decisions about the amount of news consumption that is best for us. If we are beginning to feel numb to news content, maybe we are seeing too much. We have the power to limit our viewing of 24-hour news channels as well as the number of push notifications from news media on our smartphones.

It is certainly impossible to be compassionate about every tragedy with which we come into contact. The mere idea of showing compassion towards all the bad news in our world is nothing short of overwhelming, particularly if we do not have the power to affect change for all who are suffering. As Figley states, "We have to adapt to what we are compassionate about." That adaptation comes in the form of causes and stories that are a priority to us or have touched our lives or our loved ones in a significant way. Like attention, our compassion is a finite resource, which requires us to make decisions about what is important and where we can impact the most change. We can select one cause that is most important to us and get involved. Maybe those who have a loved one who suffered from cancer might be inclined to volunteer or give to a cancer charity or research center. A family might make a commitment to support one natural disaster relief effort per year, hosting bake sales, clothing drives, and perhaps volunteering at shelters. We do not have to feel as if we should support everyone or everything, or even feel as if we should be compassionate about every single news story that comes across our screen. However, if we find one cause that is most dear to us and take action, not only can we avoid elements of compassion fatigue, but we can also feel like we are making the world a better place. We can feel empowered to do something for others in a real and tangible way. Experiencing anxiety and worry while passively sitting on the couch is not going to help anyone. Although the amount of compassion we each have is limited, there are no limits to the positive change that each of us can make if we channel our energy to the right outlet.

CHAPTER 10

Too Much Information

Ryan is a fashion designer. He leads a team that is responsible for designing activewear for a number of famous labels. His workday starts once he boards the subway into the office, reading a long list of emails that were sent overnight from factories in Asia. He scans his inbox, deciding which will be of highest priority when he arrives at the office; which can wait and be added to a to-do list; and which he can ignore after reading. Upon arriving at the office, he meets team members to review their current designs. During that 30-minute meeting, he is interrupted to answer questions regarding pricing for an upcoming meeting with a large buyer. They need clarification on three points and it cannot wait. He shifts his focus from the planning meeting with his team to focus on the points for the presentation to the buyer. He answers the questions and continues the planning discussion with his team. The meeting with the designers concludes with more discussion needed later to finalize their next steps.

It is now 10:30 and he has more emails waiting for him, many of which are follow-ups to the emails he read on his commute and to which he has yet to respond. He once again prioritizes those emails and decides which need immediate attention. In the meantime, a call from one of the sellers asks him if he has any feedback on their most recent proposal to another buyer. "It is not the nature of the work or the job, it is just the massive amount of information that is required to juggle all of the time. Sometimes I have to stop and digest the many things that I am reading, seeing, and hearing. If it comes all at once, it is almost impossible to understand it all, let alone make a decision where millions of dollars are on the line."

All of this information, coming from multiple sources, has now become the standard American workday. We bounce around from data point to data point, slowly moving towards gathering enough information to make decisions and ultimately progress in our day-to-day work. We receive information from both humans and digital sources, some of which is valuable and some not. Massive cognitive demands are placed on each of us as we attempt to sort the relevant from the irrelevant, and ultimately to make decisions based upon information that comes from multiple sources and in some cases conflict with one another. This is life in the information age.

Information is everywhere. Just over the past two years, we have generated over 90% of the data that was ever created in the history of the world. It comes in the form of emails, social media, TV, radio, podcasts, magazines, newspapers, games, Netflix, instant messaging, and a plethora of other sources and platforms. We develop and consume videos of everything from terrorist bombings to Grandma's surprise ninetieth birthday party and a host of other apps and sources, from friends to strangers to media conglomerates. In many cases we are consuming and contributing information on two or more platforms simultaneously. We can watch the news, hearing the anchor discuss the latest political news while seeing a scroll at the bottom of the screen detailing when the next hurricane is going to hit the Gulf Coast. At the same time, we can be on social media arguing with multiple people that none of the things we are seeing on the news is even happening at all! Like Ryan, we juggle multiple sources of information to prioritize and redirect our attention. The addition of more information does not necessarily mean more quality. In many cases, we have to make decisions regarding conflicting or contradictory information to somehow find the truth. We also have to sift through all of this information to determine what is relevant to us at any given time. Decades ago, information was a valuable commodity and those who possessed it were at an advantage. Today, information is everywhere and success is not just having access to it but, more importantly, determining and prioritizing what is important within a sea of the unimportant.

Information Overload

Information overload is when the amount of information available exceeds the cognitive capacity of the individual attempting to make a decision. As we discussed earlier, we are bound by our ability to cognitively process all of the information with which we engage. Our brains are designed to process small amounts of information at any given time. Too much information about a particular topic or issue impacts our ability to focus on what is most relevant. In addition, our working memory, the mental workspace that holds information long enough for us to use it, can only hold so many different items at one time. Constant exposure to more and more information can affect our concentration, creativity, and ability to remember. The most used analogy is that our working memory is like a glass and information is being poured into it like water. At some point, as information continues to be poured, it will overflow. That is kind of what our working memory is like with access to all of this information. Information just continues to overflow the glass, replacing older information with new.

The implications of this overload on our working memory are that we have difficulty functioning in basic tasks, can become stressed, and certainly lose our ability to be more productive. Think about newborn babies; the entire world around them is new. As they look around their environment, their eyes and head move from one object to another, trying to make sense of a world that has little meaning. Gradually, different experiences such as touch and food create meaning in the sights and sounds around the baby. Shapes are no longer as important as the faces of their parents or caregivers, those who provide food, touch, and care. As we grow older and experience different phenomena, we begin to search and focus on what is important, filtering out the unimportant sounds and sights around us. We function similarly as we engage new information on the internet, having difficulty knowing where to focus our attention as we make sense of massive amounts of data from both known and unknown sources. Thinking about Ryan's normal day, how does he prioritize all the different data he receives to make a plan for the day, let alone a long-term strategy?

In some ways, we have come to accept information overload as just a norm of personal and professional life. Rarely do we think about the impact of all of this information, and in many cases the technology associated with it, on our overall well-being and productivity. There is an expectation, whether societal or in the workplace, that we will engage every instant message, email, tweet, and so on that is sent to us. And we tend to meet that expectation. In the past, if you wanted to communicate with a colleague immediately, you would visit her workstation. Years later, it was easier to send an email (in many cases with a subject line like "Quick question," which I always think means "Quick answer, please"). Nowadays we want to get the attention of people even faster so we instant message them to get our quick answer (although some still stop by with the worst question ever devised in the workplace: "Did you get my email?"). It is the norm to have multiple avenues of communication and information flowing at us and from us at any given time. For decades and perhaps up until the turn of this century, the limits of our advancement have been based upon the limitations of technology and most notably the accessibility of information. How we could learn more about the world, others, and ourselves was dependent upon our ability to answer some of those basic questions through science and communicate those answers to the broader population. With this information age, our limits seem to be no longer based upon technology, but rather upon our biological capacity to understand all of this new information. Unlike the cable company that can upgrade our wiring to broadband or any other potential substance to make more data transmit faster, our brains are the same ones that our ancestors had 40,000 years ago.

Incidentally, the idea of information overload is as old as information itself. Socrates warned of the pitfalls of writing thoughts as the act would "create forgetfulness in the learners' souls, because they will not use their memories." In the centuries that followed, each generation was concerned about both the quality and the amount of information. *The Great Mirror* was created to highlight all the necessary books that one should read. Compiled by Vincent of Beauvais in the twelfth century, it took 29 years to develop and consists of 80 books and close to 10,000 chapters. Vincent himself said that the decision about what was included in *The Great Mirror* was that the works were worthy of contemplation. (He suggested books to read long before Amazon began suggesting them to us.) As the printing press was invented, many warned of the dangers of too many books. How on earth would anyone read all of these books? Many scholars also warned of the confusion that would come from so many books and even authors themselves warned that given the ease with which books could now be printed, their writings could end up in the wrong hands (unlike this book, which I hope gets into as many hands as possible). There were even fears of the democratization of knowledge where the working class might get access to knowledge that they would otherwise not possess.

As the telegraph and eventually telephone and radio came into being, the speed at which people received information accelerated greatly. Geographical barriers were broken down through instantaneous communication. With the internet and various forms of hand-held smart devices, our ability to consume and create information has risen exponentially, along with the speed by which information can be passed from one human to, in some cases, billions of other humans, all with the push of a smart device.

Managing It All

There are several symptoms of information overload. First, we have difficulty making a decision. We become so overwhelmed with choices, and information about those choices, that we become para-lyzed to a point that we may not decide anything whatsoever. Our brains have limits to where they can focus and ultimately process information. As we are being asked to process data quickly through-out the day, we may have trouble making sense of multiple data points. In some cases our working memory can become so taxed that we are constantly finding ourselves reviewing the same informa-tion over and over because we are not processing all of it. Second, information overload can create anxiety. A recent study conducted among managers around the world found that 73% felt they needed more information to perform their jobs better, but 66% reported tension with their co-workers and upper management related to information overload. In many cases, the anxiety over information overload was related to the pressure of reviewing as well as creating and sending communication within organizations.

The very notion of realizing that you do not need to engage or process all of the information that you perceive and that it does not all have to be read or comprehended is actually rather liberating. We do not have to be subjected to whatever is in front of us. We can make decisions regarding the amount of information with which we engage, and even better, be more selective in determining where we want to spend our time and attention. This does not necessarily mean that we should be ignoring emails at work, but some items are priority and some are not. Prioritization can help determine what requires an instantaneous response and what might be something that can wait until a face-to-face conversation occurs. Information should not be like the broccoli we were served as seven-year-olds; just because it is in front of us doesn't mean we have to consume it (I never ate that stuff anyway). We could feel anxiety because we're overwhelmed by all the different sources of information around us. Many feel powerless from the sense that they are flooded with emails and a constant barrage of bad news from what seem to be all angles. Dr. Sara Gorman, author of *Denying to the Grave: Why We Ignore the Facts That Will Save Us,* says that information overload can cause our brains to essentially work harder to attempt to process all the information that is coming at us. "Cognitive fatigue is associated with your brain basically working overtime to process everything. You may have a slightly harder time controlling expression of emotions or may make bad, hasty decisions. It's not entirely different in that way from just being tired (i.e., sleep deprived)."

There is a notion of both availability and volume when it comes to how we can manage information. As mentioned earlier, we must continue to manage our attention, considering how and when we should be available both to others as well as to the constant notifications that come from our computers and our phones. Through email, social media, instant notifications, and texts, we are essentially available all of the time. If we continually focus our attention on our devices, we are limiting our ability to control our own attention towards our work, communication with others, or anything else that we want and need to accomplish. Everyone has to decide what window is appropriate for responding to emails and texts, but if there is something urgent that requires your focus in your email inbox, then maybe a quick phone call to resolve the situation is the best route. Setting aside time during each day to respond to communication can help us focus on one task at a time and limit information overload. As Gorman states, "Try to circumscribe certain times of day for looking at new information/the news; this can help you avoid the kind of multitasking discussed above or the illusion that you can interrupt your workflow and dive right back in seamlessly; definitely don't look at the news at bedtime; engage in other activities that will be more focusing/rejuvenating, like physical exercise, meditation, etc."

We must also be discerning and not place the same value on each piece of information that we may receive. Emails, push notifications, text messages, and other forms of information do not all carry the same value. If we can decide which are relevant and which are not, we can begin to limit the amount of information that is coming at us. Just because it is a line in our email inbox or a push notification on our phone doesn't mean that it is important. We all can be empowered to place value on each and decide which require immediate attention, which can wait until later, and which are altogether irrelevant. Gorman also suggests that we have to be forgiving of ourselves when it comes to how we manage our consumption of information. "This moment is unusual and especially difficult so it's to be expected that some people might struggle with this. Acceptance of what you cannot entirely control is helpful in fighting feelings of being overwhelmed in general, so in this case accepting that you're not perfect and will check the news when you're not "supposed" to no matter what you do." Finally, we can also do a "brain dump" and write down all of the different tasks, information sources, or even conflicting information that we might be encountering. Through this approach, we can have all of the information sources identified in one area, which makes it all far more manageable. In many cases, it is a matter of managing the many tasks – and the barrage of information that comes along with it – rather than all of it managing you.

CHAPTER 11

FOMO

It is a cold winter night and you are settled in with your significant other to spend the evening together with takeout and Netflix. You got some Chinese food from your favorite place, you are in your jammies, and the binge-watching will soon commence. What a great night. At one point during the evening, you pick up your phone and visit Facebook or Instagram and check out the newsfeed. You see that two friends have posted videos of their vacations in the Caribbean, all of which look fabulous. The weather is great, they look great, and the drinks look way better than the boxed wine you had with your kung pao chicken. Suddenly, you are not as content with your evening as you were before you picked up the phone. You feel like you have been left out of the fun – and the sun, for that matter. You might even begin to question your choice of evening activities (or movies or food or significant others!). It is the fear of missing out, or FOMO, a term that was added to the Oxford English Dictionary in 2013 and defined as "the uneasy and sometimes all-consuming feeling that you're missing out – that your peers are doing, in the know about, or in possession of more or something better than you." It is that impression that everyone is having a much better experience, whether it's more love and happiness or just that there is some party somewhere occurring and you are not there.

FOMO is not a new phenomenon. For thousands of years, not missing out was a pretty big deal. If you missed out on the threat of a tiger roaming close by, you might miss out on tomorrow completely. If you somehow were left out of the tribe, you might not gain the benefits of protection from the other members during famine or war. Missing out on a new way to gather food, or later grow food, could have meant the difference between eating and starving. So not only is FOMO an old phenomenon, but it has been critical to our survival. The amygdala – the part of the brain that detects threats – becomes activated when we feel threatened in some way. It can activate our flight or fight response. The threat of not having vital information can be enough to trigger the amygdala. Today, we do not necessarily have those same concerns relative to basic needs, but that desire to be in the know or a part of the group still exists.

Keeping up with the Joneses

Social media is a big contributor to FOMO. Logging into Facebook or Instagram causes us to routinely see the experiences that others are posting online. As discussed earlier, we visit social media to receive attention, praise, and adulation. Many of us share our dinners, vacations, and all the job promotions and major purchases that we make in our lives. Sometimes referred to as "bragbook," Facebook, as well as other social media platforms, allow us to showcase that life is going well to impress those closest to us, or in many cases with the people we connect to on social media whom we hardly even know. Conversely, we are also recipients of others doing the exact same thing: showcasing the best version of their lives (sometimes fictitiously). A study of over 2,000 people in England found that 43% of men admitted to distorting at least some facts about themselves to make their lives seem better. In that same study, only 18% of men and 19% of women stated that their Facebook page was an overall accurate reflection of their lives. So many people are being deceptive on their social media posts, but what makes it worse is that we tend to believe what others post about their lives. This is rather counterintuitive. You would think if everyone were being dishonest then everyone would also question others' online versions of themselves on social media. Poker games are great examples. If you are constantly bluffing, you suspect others are bluffing at different times as well. It just makes sense and can be a powerful tool for a successful gambler (so I hear). It is not the case with social media. Many of us are deceptive in our own profiles, but we think that the relationships, careers, and even the lighting around others are always perfect.

The people we choose to connect with on social media can be a significant contributor to FOMO. If we know those to whom we are connected, then not only can we use social media to strengthen our relationship with the people in our lives, but we also have a better sense of their lives. We know when our uncle is overly curating his posts on Facebook because we know our uncle. We have been to his home, know his life, and know that he exaggerates things in real life, so why would Facebook be any different? But when we do not know the people to whom we are connected, that's when we may begin to experience FOMO. The disconnect between the perception of others on social media and our own lives causes us to question the choices we make. *The Smith family is so happy. I wonder if my life would've been better if I had _____ (fill in the blank here)*. In essence, we are comparing our real lives with others' curated versions of themselves. This is not fair at all. It is an impossible comparison. There is no way we know the actual lives of the Smith family. We only see what they decide to post on social media.

We all have things in our lives that we would like to improve upon, whether our appearance, our income, or even our relationships. All of us are a work in progress. However, on social media we do not always see others' work in progress. We only see the best of their lives. You rarely have people posting the extra 20 pounds they gained during the COVID-19 quarantine as a badge of honor. "Look everyone. We discovered Cheetos during COVID quarantine! Time for swimsuit photos!" Many of us post the best of ourselves. In this case, we post when we start exercising again and lose the weight from the Cheetos. That is kind of the social media challenge that each of us faces as we have all the "warts" of our real life compared to the curated version of others. Over time, that constant comparison can weigh heavily on individuals psychologically. FOMO, and its relationship to social media, can create a rather vicious cycle. So if you are unhappy psychologically, you pick up your phone and go onto social media. As you are on social media, you see all the great pictures and posts of people you know and do not know having (what appears to be) a much better life than you, which makes you feel much worse.

As you feel worse, you once again feel unhappy and turn back to social media and find more curated pictures and posts by friends and connections, which creates this vicious cycle of unhappiness.

Melissa Hunt and her colleagues explored several factors related to overall well-being between groups who were limited to 30 minutes of social media time per day against those who continued their usual social media usage over the course of three weeks. The 30 minutes was divided among three social media platforms: Facebook, Instagram, and Snapchat for 10 minutes each. After that time, the 143 participants in the study took a health survey that explored seven different outcome measures: FOMO, anxiety, depression, loneliness, social support, self-esteem, and autonomy and self-acceptance. They found that those who limited social media were less depressed and lonely. As Hunt states, "It is hugely important for people to limit the amount of social media time per day. The most appropriate use of social media is staying connected with those who you care about. Those tend to be happier, and less lonely." Spending more time on social media is putting the focus of our attention on the curated lives of other people and not on our own activities. This time can also create the habit of comparison. You have a nice evening with a friend catching up and come home and log onto Facebook and see a picture of friends lighting fireworks on a beach somewhere. The first thought is, "Wow. I thought I had a nice evening with my friend, but there were no fireworks and beaches for me. What a wasted night." Suddenly, as you start to make an unfair comparison, that nice evening with a friend was not as nice as you originally thought. In many regards, we can become audience members to the lives of others via social media. And since much of that content on social media is curated or even false, you might be watching something that is, at best, merely based on a true story. Who knew social media might need to be classified as fiction rather than nonfiction!

As Linda and Charlie Bloom, authors of *101 Things I Wish I Knew When I Got Married,* state, "There is a direct correlation between the rise in FOMO in the last decade and the spread of technology as the primary form of communication for people. Many people who have a strong desire for attention and recognition love to have others envy them. The desire for self-promotion often comes from a sense of personal insignificance. Of course, we all desire praise and attention. There is, however, a saying, 'you can never get enough of what you really don't need.' What people really need is the experience of being seen, accepted, and valued for being authentically who we are. It's like drinking saltwater: It just makes you thirstier." We may go onto social media looking to fill a void in our lives, but in so doing, we create an even larger void. Engaging on social media with those with whom we already have a genuine relationship can increase the depth of our connection. Social media can strengthen those relationships and make our connection stronger. However, if we are looking to social media to be that primary source for attention and authenticity, it can only lead us further astray.

Andrew Przybylski and his colleagues developed a 10-part questionnaire that measures FOMO. Take a shot at answering the questions below and keep track of the total number that you score at the end. The questions are as follows:

1. *I sometimes wonder if I'm spending too much time keeping up with what is going on.*
   1. Not at all 2. Just a little 3. Moderately 4. Quite a lot 5. All the time

2. *When I go on vacation or take a trip, I like to keep tabs on what my friends are doing back home.*
   1. Not at all 2. Just a little 3. Moderately 4. Quite a lot 5. All the time

3. *I fear that my friends have more rewarding experiences in their lives than me.*
   1. Not at all 2. Just a little 3. Moderately 4. Quite a lot 5. All the time

4. *When I miss out on a planned get-together, it bothers me.*
   1. Not at all 2. Just a little 3. Moderately 4. Quite a lot 5. All the time

5. *I fear others are having more rewarding experiences than me.*
   1. Not at all 2. Just a little 3. Moderately 4. Quite a lot 5. All the time

6. *It bothers me when I miss an opportunity to meet up with friends.*
   1. Not at all 2. Just a little 3. Moderately 4. Quite a lot 5. All the time

7. *I get worried when I find out my friends are having fun without me.*
   1. Not at all 2. Just a little 3. Moderately 4. Quite a lot 5. All the time

8. *I get anxious or nervous when I don't know what my friends are up to.*
   1. Not at all 2. Just a little 3. Moderately 4. Quite a lot 5. All the time

9. *It's important that I understand my friends' "in jokes."*
   1. Not at all 2. Just a little 3. Moderately 4. Quite a lot 5. All the time

10. *When I'm having a good time, it's important for me to share the details online (such as updating my status on Facebook or posting a photo on Instagram).*

    1. Not at all 2. Just a little 3. Moderately 4. Quite a lot 5. All the time

    Total: _____

How did you score? If you scored 0–14, no FOMO is likely; 15–22 you are at risk for FOMO; 23–29 is medium FOMO; and if you scored 30 and up, you are exhibiting severe FOMO. It is important to note that this is not a diagnostic quiz or professional assessment. However, as the authors note, it can be helpful for some people to talk about potential symptoms with their doctor or mental health professional.

Self-determination theory focuses on human motivation and personality as they relate to innate psychological needs. It links personality, human motivation, and optimal functioning where there is both intrinsic and extrinsic motivation. As you recall from previous chapters, intrinsic motivation comes from within, usually our internal drives that inspire us, whether our interests, values, or religious or moral upbringing. Extrinsic motivation is focused more on an external reward, such as money or food or something else that satisfies a basic need or desire. Self-determination theory refers to our ability to essentially make choices and have some element of control over our own lives. It has a profound impact on our motivation because we feel motivated to do something if we feel we can somehow impact the outcome. There are a multitude of studies that suggest that those with a high level of self-determination theory tend to be more successful. There are three innate and psychological needs that are part of self-determination theory: competence, connection, and autonomy. Competence refers to our desire to control the outcome and experience some element of mastery. For example, Deci, one of the researchers who founded the notion of self-determination theory, suggests that unexpected positive feedback on a task can enhance our intrinsic motivation to continue with the task. Connection or relatedness is our innate desire to connect with and care for others. Finally, autonomy is our desire to be the causal agents of our own lives. If we are satisfied in these three critical areas, we are less likely to experience FOMO or some of the negative psychological effects that come from viewing others' curated (or even real) lives on social media.

Freeing Ourselves from FOMO

Social media, by its very nature, entails scrolling through activities that we miss. We see the curated posts of others, and most if not all are experiences that, in some way, shape, or form we are not included in. That regular exposure to activities in which we are not participating lends itself to FOMO. Areas where we experience FOMO could be new restaurants, business opportunities, vacations, and even conversations. We may not even realize exactly what it is that we are missing, but we feel that we are missing "something." Given the daily deluge of information we all face, we are going to see something online in which we are not participating. Even if you have only five Facebook friends, you are going to see content where you have not been included. The real trigger for FOMO, however, is our own feeling of satisfaction relative to our own basic needs.

Linda and Charlie Bloom outline several practices that can help free you from FOMO. First, *slow down*. Practice taking time in performing everyday tasks, including eating, drinking, talking, brushing your teeth, driving, making love, and getting dressed. By living more mindfully, we can really recognize and more fully engage in our lives with more depth and fulfillment. It doesn't mean that everything, including taking out the garbage, is some grand activity, but in slowing down we can begin to remember that life is not a race or a contest to finish as quickly as possible, but rather a series of moments to be experienced and be informed by. The Blooms also suggest that we prioritize the items and experiences that are most valuable to us, which reminds us that life requires us to distinguish our deeper needs from our more superficial desires, and that letting go is at least as important as attaining the fulfillment of our desires, if not more so. No different than our attention, our time is of limited quantity, so prioritize what is important to you and focus on it. The Blooms also suggest that feeling a sense of gratitude can help limit the effects of FOMO. So much of our ability to limit FOMO is related to identifying experiences that bring a sense of fulfillment and genuine well-being into our lives. This form of self-reflection almost always provides a more satisfying and lasting impact on our quality of life than that which results from an obsessive pursuit of the temporary gratitude that our quest for more can ever bring!

Social media is a great outlet for communicating with those closest to us. It allows us to stay in touch with friends and relatives who may live far away. However, perception is not necessarily reality. The connections we have that are beyond the circle of people we know can create a false narrative that our real lives just cannot compete. If we can focus our attention on our lives, on both the beauty and even the warts that make up the experiences we are having, we can truly get the most out of our journey. It reminds me of the expression "Stay in your lane," which in some cases means to focus your attention on what you are doing and not on others. We all have different journeys, and peeking at the lives of others with the objective of offering some comparison is not going to help us. Besides, the worst feeling in the world may be knowing that what we missed was already right in front of us; we just didn't appreciate it when we had it. Perhaps it is time to put down the phone and return to our binge-watching and kung pao chicken.

CHAPTER

The Outrage Machine

"Anybody can become angry, that is easy; but to be angry with the right person, and to the right degree, and at the right time, and for the right purpose, and in the right way, that is not within everybody's power, that is not easy."

— Aristotle, *The Art of Rhetoric*

Garrison is an IT manager for a small government contractor and works from home. He spends about three hours per day on social media. Each day, he posts multiple times on Facebook, Twitter, and Instagram. If you want to get the latest news, he is the source. It may be a biased source, but he is current with breaking news from both trustworthy and perhaps not-so-trustworthy sources. Most of his posts are political in nature, arguing about both policies as well as moral and religious issues with friends and complete strangers. It seems as if every time I see him, he has blocked a relative over some heated argument. (I guess they unblock each other after they cool down a bit and the cycle continues.) When I ask him why he continually participates in these arguments, he says, "I just can't let it go. They are so wrong in what they are saying and believing and it just bothers me to a point that I need to respond."

I often wonder if people really think that all of this time arguing on social media is really serving them. Once in a while I have discussed certain topics on social media and never during any of them has anyone ever said, "That is a really good point. I never thought of it that way. I am glad we had this dialogue." In the spirit of full disclosure, I have never said that to anyone else either. We just seem so pissed off all the time, and it is something different each day and perhaps every hour. Twitter is always "blowing up" in response to what someone said or some terrible slight at an awards show or something even more trivial! People regularly take to social media to voice their outrage. Once the responses start pouring it, let the games begin. The feud is on, whether between the right and the left, the sports fans wearing green versus those in purple, right-handed people versus left-handed, whatever. Incidentally, researchers in Australia found that the angriest tweets tend to come on Mondays (not a surprise) and as weather gets colder, the tweets also tend to get meaner. Combine a gaffe on a reality television show with a cold Monday and you have the components for a high-powered outrage machine.

The *Urban Dictionary* describes outrage culture as "When people play the victim card and bend over backwards to be as offended as possible when they really aren't." Tim Kreider of the *New York Times* first penned the term in 2009, stating, "It seems as if most of the news consists of outrage porn, selected specifically to pander to our impulses to judge and punish and get us all riled up with righteous indignation." That seems abundantly true. Moral outrage is good for business. If we are upset about something, there is a higher likelihood that we will engage with the topic. We outlined media platforms' motivation for clickbait in Chapter 3. You know the standard clickbait headlines: "You will be shocked at what politician X said yesterday!" or "We now know how much money person Z has and it will surprise you!" How do they know we will be surprised? Seems like a bit of an assumption; maybe we already know. Nevertheless, outrage brings clicks and eyeballs on cable news, websites, and social media. Cable news channels strive for and achieve outrage through opinion and sensationalism, keeping the viewer engaged and enraged for as long as possible.

Threats always seem to be a good strategy. The threats of foreign invaders, lawlessness, or elimination of basic rights always cause alarm and the media and opinion regularly push that button, particularly on the evening cable news shows. Social media platforms want engagement for as long as possible as well. Their strategy is to use algorithms that will continue to serve you content based upon what you engaged with before as well as echo chambers that we will address later. I have been part of several groups on Facebook and it seems as if the emerging objective of so many of them is to highlight each ridiculous comment or action from both known and unknown people, pointing out how awful it was that a pastor in the middle of somewhere said this thing, or that someone at a rally had this terrible sign. We find ourselves immersed in outrage, and social media gives us the platform to be as angry as we want about just about anything. Once again, the sources of information that we consume have a different objective than we do. More outrage means more engagement and more engagement means more eyeballs to advertisers.

Did You See That?!

The notion of responding negatively to news is not a new phenomenon. Decades ago, people would shake their fist at the TV, write angry letters to politicians and celebrities, and vent or complain to anyone who would listen. However, before the advent of social media, everyone did not have a large platform to vent their frustrations about current events. They might discuss topics, rationally or angrily, with friends and family members. Although that dialogue probably wasn't always polite or even useful, there was indeed conversation, a sharing of perspectives, and people were largely working under the same set of facts.

Up until the 1980s, people tended to get their news from merely a handful of sources, whether it was the broadcast channels or their local newspapers and radio. Today, there are countless sources for news and information with varying levels of credibility. We can be tweeting our outrage while watching news that is making us outraged, not thinking carefully about what we are saying or how we are saying it. Dr. Michael Griffin, professor of media studies at Macalester College and author of *Media and Community*, says, "Certainly people felt outrage in the face of atrocities, malfeasance, political incompetence or betrayal, or simply boorish behavior before the advent of the World Wide Web and social media. But pre-internet outrage built more slowly (over months and years of fear, frustration and grieving over the conduct of the Vietnam War, for example, or over days watching the Watergate hearings on television) and tended to develop and be expressed after longer periods of consideration and often more indirectly (spending days or weeks organizing a protest march, for example, or by voting against the offending political candidate in the next election). The web and social media, for the first time in history, affords large numbers of people the ability to express their displeasure or condemnation immediately, even tweeting about statements and events in real time as they are happening." If we feel a sense of outrage over an event in real time, we can respond immediately and even pile on to others' responses. If we are responding to live events in real time with our friends and connections on social media where like-minded people are showing outrage simultaneously, a gang mentality can emerge, where emotions can begin to take priority over rational thought. Just as bad, our ability to post our outrage instantaneously can lead to responses that we might regret later. We all know of instances where individuals have lost their jobs or businesses because of a tweet or Facebook post. Many advocate for the need to think before tweeting or posting, which is certainly good advice.

In 2014, *Slate* published the Year of Outrage, an interactive calendar of the topics that made us riled up over the course of the year. As the authors write, "People were upset about TV stars and wheelchairs and lattes and racism and war." As I examined each of the days of the calendar of that year, it is difficult to remember much of any of the incidents that caused such outrage. There were important events that year, such as the happenings in Ferguson, Missouri, and others related to war, the economy, and human rights. However, the large majority of events that fueled outrage were events that are completely meaningless (such as John Travolta mispronouncing Idina Menzel's name at the Oscars; oh, the humanity). Yet thousands if not millions of people invested time and energy in tweeting and posting their frustration over a myriad of trivial occurrences. Worse yet is the harmful rhetoric that comes from this outrage culture, sometimes creating abusive language on social media or even causing fragmentation among families and friends. And for what? There are certainly cases where outrage created good, whether through protest or contacting political officials about important decisions that impact people's lives. However, given our culture, that is now the exception, not the norm.

Dr. Keith Campbell, professor in the Department of Psychology at the University of Georgia, suggests that social media is a bit of a breeding ground for narcissism that lends itself to outrage. There is a constant reinforcement of self-promotion, identity, and less than authentic relationships. When you are fully engaged in social media, you are participating in an attention economy where individuals are developing content, pictures, and posts, link-sharing and commenting, all to attract as much attention as possible. Our motivation to express outrage can be related to likes on social media. If we are living in a filter bubble with people of a similar mindset, we can gain attention from others if we are the ones who are highlighting moral superiority or just plain anger. If it is "the other side" politically, we have an opportunity to gain approval from those within our circle for being upset over some small action or episode. We can also express outrage anonymously on social media. We can use Twitter to showcase our outrage without identifying ourselves, picking fights with those who disagree with our outrage.

And it feels so good to be outraged. Researchers at New York University examined over 500,000 communications on Twitter and found that the use of moral and political words increased the likelihood of those communications being spread by 20% for each additional word added to the communication. So discussions about topics related to morality and politics can spread like wildfire on Twitter, bringing new outrage and rhetoric. As Griffin states, "The ability to express reactions and opinions immediately, combined with the capacity to share and circulate commentary with contacts across social networks very quickly, facilitates the sharing and spread of 'outrage' at great speed across large networks of people. The high speed and broad reach of such communications also gives these messages a sense of urgency, promoting participation, response, and reposting/retweeting of messages. Cumulatively, this serves both to extend participation and to intensify emotional reactions, particularly because it happens online, in virtual space, where people are conveniently shielded from face-to-face interactions with others." In addition, the spread of these communications was within like-minded groups, potentially causing more polarization for reasons discussed in earlier chapters.

Campbell also suggests that there are a number of angry and scared people who find themselves drawn towards social media. As he states, "With many people, there is real fear, vulnerability, and anxiety. That manifests itself into aggression, anger, and hostility. People are feeling kind of empty for one reason or another and there is real fear that lends itself to outrage." There is a cycle of anxiety that social media brings us. When we are anxious, we tend to be more vigilant. Think about our ancestors centuries ago trying to fend off predators. They also could have been anxious to find food while hunting, fearing that they would potentially starve to death. This vigilance served our ancestors well. Today, our brains are still wired to be vigilant during anxiety, causing us to reach for our phones and check social media or respond to some push notification or news event. Algorithms within sites like Facebook, Twitter, and YouTube serve us more content that is consistent with what likely made us outraged in the first place, leading to more reinforcement. Accessing sites like Twitter with various threats and negativity can create more anxiety, and thus the cycle of negativity and anxiety is born.

The calmest, most thoughtful voices are not likely going to be the ones who are going to gain the most attention on social media or even on cable news. It is going to be difficult to gain attention online if we are saying, "Everything is great, no need to panic," or "This is a complicated issue so let's not rush to judgment." If the goal is to gain eyeballs, then there is a motivation to rush to judgment, to tell us the other side is bad, or to scare the daylights out of everyone so they will stay tuned in and logged on. Obviously, rushing to judgment is never a good thing. In many cases, we are talking about complicated policy issues or, at minimum, a person's livelihood and reputation. Second, if we are constantly screaming that there is an emergency just for the sake of attracting attention, what happens when there is actually an emergency? Will anyone listen? It is the equivalent of sitting in a movie theatre and hearing someone scream "fire" multiple times. After three or four screams, you start to tune it out. But what happens if the twelfth person screaming "fire" actually sees a fire?

Jillian Jordan and her colleagues explored why individuals would become upset or even act if there is some sort of injustice, even when they are not the victim. Through a series of economic game experiments, they found that third party punishers – those who respond in some way to those who may have committed some offense against someone else – gain trustworthiness by signaling some sort of offense. So we can gain credibility by chastising others on social media for offenses large and small. We could also potentially be gaining credibility from like-minded individuals within our echo chambers. For example, if someone makes a racial or homophobic slur in a public forum, people's motivation to respond with outrage is to advertise that they themselves are not racist or homophobic.

In some cases, the moral outrage can actually backfire. Two researchers at Stanford University showed over 3,000 people social media posts that had caused some sort of outrage, such as the famous selfie in front of the concentration camp and other controversial posts. They then asked participants to read some of the actual social media responses to these posts. Participants didn't express any less condemnation for the post, but they also felt sympathy for the poster, thinking that the response to the action was disproportionate. It didn't even matter whether the person was high profile or not. If the post was incredibly offensive, there was outrage. However, there was also a feeling of sympathy for the poster. The study does not take into consideration the response if there are thousands of posts of outrage about an incident. It is possible that a universal reaction of outrage could impact bystanders' levels of sympathy. However, the response to the response, if you will, seems to depend upon what outraged posters' motivations are for piling on. If the motivation is to persuade others to feel similarly, then it may not have the desired effect.

Tired of "Sick and Tired"

Being exposed to news and information that causes some sort of outrage is nothing short of overwhelming. We cannot go each and every day feeling frustrated and, well, outraged. As we discussed earlier, compassion fatigue occurs when we experience emotional or physical exhaustion from caregiving or merely constant exposure to bad news or witnessing the suffering of others. Similarly, outrage fatigue can occur when we find ourselves continually at our maximum when it comes to outrage or response to what we believe is a transgression of some sort. Our ability to address compassion fatigue requires us to pick a topic or two that we feel most passionate about and devote some of our time and energy to that topic. If, for example, the issue you feel most passionate about is the treatment of animals in a local shelter, then consider volunteering or adopting an animal to try to make a difference. Getting involved can give us the opportunity to fix a problem that is bothering us but also empowerment in knowing that we can make a difference in the world.

Like other issues that we have addressed throughout this book, getting out of our filter bubbles and echo chambers is vitally important. Staring at cable news or Twitter all day, listening, becoming outraged and anxious alone is not likely going to be useful to us or eliminate the source of our outrage. We can perform a cognitive override, where we intellectually and rationally examine whether this outrage, or the sites and platforms that are causing it, are really in our best interests. It is not an easy task, as our emotions, habits, and perhaps even dopamine are luring us back into this cycle. However, if we can objectively examine whether we are creating a positive environment for ourselves, we may make behavioral changes that can remove us from this cycle of outrage. Campbell says, "The best way to get out of the cycle of outrage is to disconnect entirely. I try to get off the grid for at least one full week per year. That longer period of time allows me to get perspective on how important, or perhaps unimportant, many of the matters that seem to outrage us might be." Not only can time offer perspective regarding what this cycle of outrage might provide us, but it can also help us think about the importance of the things that upset us from a longitudinal perspective. As Campbell says, "Take a look back at the things that upset you a year, a month, even a week ago and evaluate how important it really is. You can look at some of the things you posted on Facebook and Twitter and ask, 'Why was I so invested in something so meaningless now? Was it really worth it?'"

Being active rather than passive is the best way to feel as if we are making a difference in the world, as opposed to merely ruminating about it or merely arguing with strangers on social media. Campbell suggests that you can make a commitment to equal the amount of time you spend online with time offline, volunteering for a local charity, spending time playing basketball with the neighborhood kids, or becoming a mentor of some sort. There is real power in balancing this virtual reality machine with doing something real and meaningful. Perhaps most importantly, you can channel this anxiety and even the anger into something positive that can make you feel as if you are making a difference. And, at the end of the day, how outraged should we actually be about all of these things? Sure, there are real problems in the world that require an active, informed public engaged as voters, community members, and volunteers. We certainly need more involvement and activism to make this world a better place. At the same time, if you find yourself on Twitter and feeling burned out, angry, or depressed all the time, it might be time to reevaluate. As Campbell suggests, "If you find that all of these things are consuming you, you should examine it carefully and figure out if it is working for you. Even in the worst-case scenario where the world falls apart, you don't have to feel bad all day about it. Workout or better yet, bake a cake." Keeping it all in perspective is valuable advice for us all. If the outrage is becoming too overwhelming and you do decide to head to the kitchen to bake, I will have devil's food, please.

CHAPTER 13

Tribalism

"Loyalty to any one sports team is pretty hard to justify, because the players are always changing, the team can move to another city. You're actually rooting for the clothes when you get right down to it. You know what I mean? You are standing and cheering and yelling for your clothes to beat the clothes from another city. Fans will be so in love with a player, but if he goes to another team, they boo him. This is the same human being in a different shirt; they hate him now. Boo! Different shirt! Boo!"

—Jerry Seinfeld, *Seinfeld*

We develop all kinds of tribes, whether with our neighbors, within our church, motorcycle club, racial and ethnic background, sexual orientation, sports teams, and of course, politics. From afar, I always felt that smokers were a pretty cohesive group, standing outside in all types of weather, talking during their breaks or lunches while getting some nicotine. There always seemed to be a bond there with that group, maybe because they have been somewhat ostracized and literally put in a place of their own. I am not advocating for or against smoking, but sometimes I am jealous of the tribal bond that smokers seem to have with one another. We instinctively search for a common bond with others who share similar interests and characteristics. Tribalism can facilitate a great sense of belonging to others, and within organizations can foster a good work environment and collaboration, among others. We have had tribal instincts for ages. Upon birth, we as humans have always been unable to take care of ourselves so our family and those around us provide for our care. They give us food, shelter, and protection from predators as well as teach us basic principles that the family and the community share. Growing up within that circle, we feel a sense of belonging in that shared culture and as we get older, we have traditionally cared for those within the tribe who could not care for themselves, whether the sick, very old, or very young. For the most part, our communities consisted of smaller groups of people who held a common ancestor. Given that transportation was limited, smaller groups had their own identities relative to food, traditions, and even religious beliefs. As we have evolved and advanced technologically, there are still tribes within communities, regions, and nations that hold some sort of common bond and sense of belonging for those who are part of it.

"My Tribe Is Better Than Yours"

As an undergraduate student, I marched in my college marching band. You would think that the group of 325 members would be the entire tribe, traveling and working together on a regular basis. And perhaps so, but there were also factions within the larger group. As the tuba players, we always felt we were more important (and in a delusional sense that we were far more attractive) than the trombone or trumpet section. In American politics, although all are Americans and share the same citizenship, and in many cases the same life goals for themselves and their families, the right and left have always had distinct differences when it comes to just about everything. The difference now is that it is not as substantive and focused on specific values or facts. As George Packer writes, "American politics today requires a word as primal as 'tribe' to get at the blind allegiances and huge passions of partisan affiliation. Tribes demand loyalty, and in return, they confer the security of belonging." There is an attitude that "you are with us or against us" when it comes to political discourse. In our dialogue, the Constitution is not cited to unite under a common cause, but rather, to throw in the face of the opposing tribe. Kind of like the tuba section's rivalry with the trombone section, except the stakes are far higher.

Tribalism

Michael Spivey, professor of cognitive science at the University of California-Merced, says, "Tribalism is always influencing our lives, but it is usually at a subconscious level. Every once in a while, with hot-button issues, it breaches the surface and becomes conscious and obvious . . . perhaps more so in the past few years. People regularly argue over political, cultural, or racial conflicts that are clearly rooted in that tribal affiliation. The moment that argumentation becomes illogical or based upon false claims, it is apparent that the conflict is actually motivated not by legitimate concerns (e.g., jobs, the economy, crime, etc.) but instead by tribalism. This is because the tribalism was always there, just usually under the surface. Cognitive scientists refer to it as implicit bias, where someone can be prejudiced about some out-group without even realizing it, often genuinely believing that they are not prejudiced at all." The notion of implicit bias can have an impact on any aspect of human life where some decision is being made that affects other people, whether law enforcement, hiring practices, student admissions, and a host of other areas. While most of us associate with some in-group, a social group where we somehow identify as being a member, our prejudice towards the out-group can manifest itself in many ways and usually starts early in life and can be amplified through media and news coverage.

Basking in reflected glory (BIRG) is a state of mind where an individual associates himself with a winner, so the winner's success becomes his success. In 1976, Cialdini and his colleagues noted the apparel of students at seven different universities on the days following football games. Students were dressed in the apparel of their school far more after a win than after a loss. Perhaps more importantly, students used the term "we" more often when referencing the win ("we won") and "they" after a loss ("they lost"). We like to associate ourselves with winning and success – even if we had nothing to do with that winning or success. We love to brag about the famous people from our hometown or perhaps the celebrity alumni from our alma maters, as if we had something to do with any of their accomplishments. With social media, we now have the opportunity to share what we like and the groups that we participate in with the world. We have the opportunity to say that "we won" or "we were right" or "we did it," when in reality, we might not have done anything, except of course, post that we did.

There are a number of sources of this amplified tribalism today in politics. As Megan A. Duncan, assistant professor in the College of Liberal Arts and Human Sciences at Virginia Tech, says, "Partisan politics has always been about values. What direction do you want the country to head in? But, this has been amped up by the rhetoric of elites in the past few election cycles. Many seemingly non-partisan issues have been co-opted by a political party by connecting it with a fundamental part of your identity. When partisan affiliations and stances on issues get tied to your identity so closely, it's more difficult to consider alternative views or change your view." In addition, we not only become isolated within our own tribes online, but in many cases move into our homogenous groups within communities as well. As Duncan states, "Political identity is associated with the population density of the place you live. So you're less likely to meet people who are different than you. That can lead toward bitterness, resentment and a lack of empathy toward other groups." If we do not see those different than us on a regular basis, then it is much more difficult to humanize them, realizing that by and large they have the same goals and aspirations for themselves and their families like we do. Duncan also points to social media as a new window into others' political leanings that we may not have seen before, causing more factions within families and communities. "You might not have known before social media what the folks who you work next to, worship with or bump into at your kids' school think about politics. That's not usually a topic of polite small talk. But, with social media platforms you get a peek into this other dimension of these folks, and you might not like what they have to say. It can mean that most relationships you have get sorted into us vs. them on political partisanship." As we'll discuss in detail in a later chapter, algorithms, whether on social media or YouTube, continue to feed us more of what they think we want, further solidifying views and putting us into filter bubbles that cause further polarization.

I had the good fortune of watching one of the 2016 U.S. presidential debates at Caesar's Palace in Las Vegas. The debate was being shown on dozens of walls of large-screen TVs between slot machines and buffets (perhaps there were wagers placed on how many times a candidate would take a sip of water or clear their throat during the debate). There were probably 150 of us watching and listening to the two candidates go back and forth over issues related to climate change, race relations, and economic strategy. What was so surprising about the response of those watching along with me wasn't the number of people who supported either candidate, but rather the cheers and boos for the different candidates after they spoke. This was not a debate to learn about the candidate's position on important issues facing the country. It was a sporting event. Everyone seemed to have a team and was rooting for their side to be the victor; in this case, the team was the candidate. It makes one wonder: if this is truly the case with everyone during these debates, why have them? If it is to be treated as a sporting event, it seems useless since there is no score or tally (or, thank goodness, choke-holds) at the end. It is easy to assume that as you read, you might be thinking, "The other side politically (or the other fan base) is far more tribal than mine." In reality, both liberals and conservatives are equally biased. In a meta-analysis of multiple studies exploring bias in both liberals and conservatives, Peter Ditto and colleagues found that both liberals and conservatives exhibited a similar level of partisan bias and pro-tribe tendencies. They also suggest that political bias tends to be more pronounced for topics that are most important to the tribe (issues such as abortion for the right; climate change for the left). Since, as they describe it, both tribes tend to equally value facts, the issues that are most likely to create bias are ones where the truth is somewhat ambiguous.

Our social identity shapes our perspective and behaviors. We see benefit in being part of a communal group that will accept us and in some cases protect us. We want our tribe to be the most dominant. When there is an element of fear involved, then this tribalism can become even more pronounced. When we feel threatened, it alters how we respond. Vladas Griskevicius and colleagues from the University of Minnesota found that our emotion impacted whether we conform or want to stand out from the crowd. They asked people to watch either a romantic or a scary film. Afterwards, people viewed ads that were rooted in conformity ("over a million sold") or uniqueness ("stand out from the crowds"). The people who watched a scary movie were more likely persuaded by a conformity-based ad, whereas those who watched the romantic film were likely to want to stand out from the crowd. When we are scared, we are more likely to want to conform to the safety of the tribe rather than stand out. I automatically envision the herd of zebras running through the safari being chased by the lion. The last thing one of the zebras want is to stand out from the pack, because standing out could mean lights out for the zebra!

Breaking Down What Divides Us

So how do we rid ourselves of these tribal instincts and be more objective in evaluating news and information, as well as engaging those who are different than us? Spivey says, "The best way to diffuse tribalism is to get people from different cultures, races, and political leanings to get exposed to each other regularly. (For example, the social engineering in Singapore, despite its drawbacks, has successfully made people less tribalistic because different cultures and races are forced to live near one another.) When a prejudiced person finds himself in a situation where he's making dozens of exceptions to his stereotype about an out-group – as in 'he's one of the good ones,' and 'she's one of the good ones' and 'he is too' – eventually the usefulness of that stereotype (with its too many exceptions) fades over time."

However, the current landscape of both news and social media today make it easy for us to become more tribal, particularly as it relates to politics and race. As Spivey says, "The ecology of social media technology has become so incredibly diverse now that it is frighteningly easy for a prejudiced person to surround themselves only with news and entertainment that rabidly promotes their tribalism instead of diffusing it. Due to the formation of these "echo chambers," where people don't ever have to hear differing perspectives, technology in the twenty-first century has undone many of the advances toward social harmony that technology in the 1970s had started." We can block information sources and other humans who do not share a similar belief to ours. According to Pew Research, a supermajority of both Republicans and Democrats view each other as "close-minded" and Republicans see Democrats as "unpatriotic." In that same study, 73% of respondents said that not only could they not agree on future plans and policies, they cannot even agree on basic facts! Surrounding ourselves with only those who are like-minded can not only impact our ability to have a balanced understanding of basic current events, but it can also cause us to think those who see it differently are the enemy, even if they are people with the same background living in the same community. Each of us sees the impact this tribalism is having on our workplaces and extended families. You do not have to look too far on social media to read about people who have declared that they cannot be friends with members of another political party or that the only thing that "the other side" is interested in is tearing down our country for one reason or another. These actions and this type of behavior cannot possibly help us find any type of common ground as communities or a nation. Duncan suggests that a little empathy goes a long way in seeing others who have different opinions and worldviews. "We all have a tendency to think that if someone only knew what we know they would have the same opinion as us. That isn't true. Developing opinions is a complicated process. Treating people who think differently with a sense of curiosity about how they came to that decision is a great way to approach an opinion difference." She also suggests that we can each be critical of our own dogma, questioning whether we are searching for balanced and objective views on topics and whether we have insulated ourselves within our own tribes. As she states it, "People have a tendency to see bias against them when there isn't one. If two people invested in an issue from opposite perspectives read a news story, both are likely to say the journalist was unfair to their views. Meanwhile, someone who has little salience to the issue will read the story as balanced toward both views. Taking a breath before you come to a decision or express your opinion gives you a moment to think about your biases and see the issue from another perspective."

Since our bias is indeed implicit, we must work harder to monitor what we say and how we say it. Spivey suggests that in addition to catching yourself when you feel, say, or do implicitly biased things, there's more that you can do. Compensate for all the implicitly prejudiced things you inevitably will do. Donate to charitable foundations that protect minority groups in your area, such as the Southern Poverty Law Center, the American Indian College Fund, the NAACP, or the Immigrant Justice Corps. It's a little bit like paying a carbon offset when you fly on an airline. The maddening thing about implicit bias is that it is implicit. This means that you are going to do and say culturally and racially biased things without even realizing it. There's no getting around that, precisely because it is implicit, but you can counter that bias by donating time and money to worthy causes that may be victimized by years of bias from others.

We can continue to monitor and question our echo chambers and search for multiple sources of news and information, whether related to sports or politics. As Duncan states, "So much of the slide toward polarization comes from policies and cues from elites/elected officials. To the extent that political candidates use increasingly polarized language, that elected officials show decreasing respect for the humanity of people with different political views, that news media give space to conspiracy theories, or that lawmakers have allowed social media platforms to operate largely unregulated, these things set the tone for normal behavior toward each other." The people on the other side of the aisle or those living or loving in a different way than perhaps our own are humans with the same feelings and goals for themselves and their loved ones. We can regularly remind ourselves that although disagreement is healthy, we all do indeed have common ground in what we hold dear in this life. Diversity of thought and experience, looking at the same challenges from different lenses, is a good thing. The other party, team, or out-group isn't the enemy that is inherently out to hurt us, but the tribalism that is part of our everyday lives today surely isn't doing us any favors.

CHAPTER 14

Instant Gratification

I run a lot. I try to log four or five days a week. Those of you who are fellow runners know that it is not always easy. The act of setting aside the time and putting on the running shorts and shoes can be a challenge in and of itself. As the run starts, the first mile is usually the toughest, but as you go, the legs start to acclimate once again and the runner's high commences. You're flying high, effortlessly gliding along hitting your target pace. As time goes on and the energy starts to deplete, the wall that you will soon hit is coming into view (As time goes on and your energy starts to diminish, that "wall" begins to approach). You push through to finish so that the next morning, you can look yourself in the mirror and face that bathroom scale. Done! What a great feeling! After the run, a funny thing happens on the way to the protein shake. A bakery pulls out in front of you and interrupts your entire plan. One of those bakeries that makes large cookies, sometimes served hot if you time it correctly. I go in, sweaty from the run, and I order two. All of that running can be undone in a savory, gooey, dopamine high. It is so good. To heck with the scale, I will face that tomorrow! Unlike my potential weight loss, which could take weeks, months, or years, the cookies are a definite satisfaction that can happen right now. I will deal with the scale tomorrow, but at this moment, it is all about instant gratification.

Instant gratification is the desire to immediately experience fulfillment without any delay. It is the temptation to focus on a short-term benefit at the expense of something more long-term. We see this in so many aspects of our lives, from food to health to sex. Technology makes it easy to get what we want – right now. Once we decide that we want something, the urge or desire can be met at the push of a button. Want food? Grubhub can deliver it. How about a ride somewhere? Uber or Lyft have you covered. Need to be entertained? There are YouTube, Netflix, and dozens of other streaming services. Our curiosity can be satisfied on a whim, too. We have a question about something, and we can immediately turn to Google or Alexa or Siri to give us the information that we need (or in some cases, the information we think we need). Communication is the same way. We email or text and expect a response immediately. If there is no immediate response, we begin to question if there is something wrong. Pornography gives us unlimited opportunity to satisfy basic urges with images of beautiful-looking people. We do not have to wait to satisfy that urge (or even buy another person dinner). The information age does certainly lend itself to instant gratification.

I Want It Now!

We have come to expect fast internet, same-day delivery, and answers to even complicated issues quickly. Ramesh Sitaraman from UMass Amherst examined the data of 6.7 million online users and found that they begin to abandon videos that do not load after just two seconds, with 6% of users leaving the video for every additional second it takes to load it. According to a survey by the Nielsen Norman Group, most users stay on a single webpage long enough to read only 20% of the text on that page. Hadar and his colleagues compared heavy users and nonusers of smartphones and found that the heavy users were much more impulsive than the nonusers. They suggest that the devices have the ability to capture attention and regularly gratify the desire for immediate rewards, and thus impact impulsivity. In 2015, Fifth Third Bank conducted an impatience survey and found that 96% of Americans will knowingly consume hot food or drink that will burn their mouth, with 63% doing so repeatedly! And 72% of Gen Yers admit to already pushing a lit elevator button as they wait. Over 50% hung up the phone after being on hold for one minute or less. They check their phones an average of eight times when waiting to hear back from someone they've dated. Incidentally, Fifth Third Bank's new ad campaign was titled "Escape the Wait." Seems like a smart idea.

So where does technology fit in with our habit of expecting instant gratification? Hal Hershfield, associate professor of Marketing and Behavioral Decision Making at UCLA's Anderson School of Management, says, "We have technology that makes it even easier for us to, well, succumb to instant gratification: If I want to watch a movie, I can just scan my face, my thumb, or click a button – no longer do I have to get in the car and go to the video rental store. There are just that many more opportunities for the normal consumer behavior friction to be lessened, and that makes it hard to fully exhibit self-control." If we had to leave our home, we might find ways to talk ourselves out of that dinner out or time allotment to watch movies. We might decide to cook for ourselves, exercise, or call a loved one instead of binge-eating Grubhub and binge-watching Netflix. Any time that we succumb to instant gratification, our brain pathways are reinforced and strengthened, and it becomes more and more difficult to break these patterns. This is important because most of the foods, purchases, and behaviors that tend to promote instant gratification are not good for our health, whether poor eating (see cookies above) or lack of exercise (binge-watching *The Crown* instead of time at the gym). They also may not be good for our wallets if we are achieving instant gratification through shopping. As we will discuss in Chapter 17, rarely are impulse buys good ones.

Humans have benefited from this desire for instant gratification for thousands of years for our very survival. Back then, as hunters, we didn't think about our prey the way we select Christmas trees: "Well, I think this bison is nice, but let's see if there are bigger ones on the other side of the river." We instantly went after dinner that was in front of us, knowing that if we didn't get something in the moment when it was available, dinner might not be served at all (there was no fridge then and certainly no Uber Eats). That innate desire to satisfy hunger made us act in the moment so we could eat, drink, and reproduce. Although our lives are dramatically different now, that primitive desire for instant gratification is still part of our hardwired brains today. Researchers used functional magnetic resonance imaging (fMRI) on 14 students at Princeton University and found that when the participants had the opportunity for an immediate reward, the part of the brain that is closely associated with emotion was activated, as opposed to the portion of the brain associated with abstract reasoning. The researchers suggest that as we get closer to a short-term reward, like dieters seeing cake or those trying to quit smoking smelling the cigarette smoke, the emotional portion of our brain tends to win the battle with the abstract reasoning portion of the brain.

Researchers at Tel Aviv University explored the effects of smoking deprivation and the anticipation of smoking on flight attendants. They asked participants who were either light or heavy smokers to identify their craving to smoke during different points in both long and short flights. They found that the craving to smoke was related to the time remaining in the flight as opposed to the time that had elapsed in the flight (or even the amount of time since the flight attendant had the last cigarette). Essentially, the flight attendants' knowledge that the flight was concluding – and thus the upcoming opportunity to smoke – led to higher cravings. The length of the flights didn't matter; it was the cue and the expectation that fueled the craving. Think about all of the cues that we have related to technology. It could be as simple as sitting on the couch and expecting the television to be on or perhaps anticipating that we will receive texts or push notifications when our phones are on and with us. As we discussed in earlier chapters, the dopamine kicks in as we sense those cues where we are close to a short-term reward.

Freud identified the pleasure principle, which is our innate desire for immediate pleasure and the avoidance of pain. He suggested that it was a significant part of the id, which is the part of the personality that focuses on our basic and instinctual needs and desires. As he suggested, the pleasure principle is with us at birth, but as we mature, we begin to see the benefit of delayed gratification relative to any number of personal wants and desires. This is most evident in the behavior of young children as they act upon their needs for hunger or thirst or other innate desires. As we get older, (hopefully) elements of our personality take over and we control some of those urges. For example, it is perfectly understandable for a two-year-old to cry over not getting the food she wants right away. However, as an adult, it might not be acceptable to throw a tantrum during a meeting when you are hungry (although the thought has clearly crossed my mind at times). As we all know, giving in to our immediate impulses for instant gratification is not likely to help us in achieving a rewarding career, strong interpersonal relationships, or a healthy lifestyle.

A Bird in the Hand . . .

In some cases, the uncertainty of a long-term reward can make us more prone to accepting something less in the short term. Many people have varying levels of risk tolerance when it comes to long-term rewards and will "play it safe" with the opportunity in front of them rather than consider something bigger in the distant future. For example, Colleen is selling her truck. She could use the extra money to pay for a few home improvements and wants to sell before the vehicle gets too old. She has a buyer for the vehicle who will pay about $3,000 less than the value of the truck. Regardless of her family's encouragement to put the truck on the market to get the actual value, Colleen is going to sell it for less. "I can get the money now and not have to take a risk of not getting it for whatever reason on the market. A bird in hand is worth two in the bush." The future is uncertain so longer-term payoffs or rewards are uncertain, compelling us to take the "now," usually in the form of less than what we need or desire.

Celeste Kidd from the University of Rochester did a different take on Mischel's famous marshmallow experiment. The children were once again promised a second marshmallow if they did not consume the first one when the researcher departed the room. However, half of the children who did resist eating the marshmallow were not given the treat, but instead, given an apology. Essentially, they were told that although they were promised a treat for holding out, there wasn't a second marshmallow available. During the second portion of the experiment where children were once again promised a second marshmallow if they did not eat the first one when the researcher left the room, most who were given the promised marshmallow the first time around held out again for the second marshmallow the second time. However, the children who were deceived the first time opted not to wait for the marshmallow this time around. They almost immediately ate the marshmallow when the researcher left the room. Just like my running and the cookies, the longer-term reward is unknown but the short-term is tangible and guaranteed, leading to less likelihood of delaying gratification.

The present is where our attention, and ultimately our expectation, lies, leaving us susceptible to the "now" as opposed to the "later." As Hershfield says, "Part of the problem here is that the present is just an incredibly powerful force on our emotions. Everything

115

that happens right now simply feels like it's more important, more emotionally powerful, and more motivating than anything that will happen in the future. We may recognize that we will feel largely the same in two years, say, than we do right now. But, two years (or five, 10, whatever length of time) just feels a lot further away, and we can convince ourselves that we can deal with the consequences later." The investment of our time and attention towards short-term, instant gratification can lead us to a pattern of inauthentic rewards.

As we discussed in previous chapters, our habits of distraction, whether social media, online gaming, or any other platform that provides us dopamine hits in the form of likes and other inauthentic attention, are likely to come at the expense of our long-term goals. Where do we see our careers, relationships, and health in the months and years ahead? Taking these goals from the abstract to concrete can help us allocate our attention towards those goals and away from the attention traps that steal so much of our focus. Three or more hours of screen time per day adds up, and given the finite nature of our attention, it all comes at the expense of something else. Instead of considering distant rewards that can come from our focus on our work or relationships, we can have smaller goals related to achieving a portion of those goals that will not only lead us in the right direction towards those longer-term goals, but give us a tangible payoff that is soon and accessible. Repeating that approach over the course of days, weeks, and months can eventually lead to long-term successes.

We can also find ways to manage our environment, whether through elimination of the chocolate cake and cigarettes in our homes, or by putting the smartphone in another room. If we can eliminate the presence of some of these cues, we have a better chance of not giving in to the parts of our brains associated with emotion and thus succumb to instant gratification. Hershfield says, "We can try to be aware of and limit situations where we know that we will fail. Are there times of day when I am 'weaker'? Are there social situations where I know I'll go beyond my financial budget? If I can recognize those settings and be aware of them, it might help me stick to my goals. Note that being aware doesn't mean avoiding. Perhaps I know that when I get tired, I'm likely to overeat or overspend, or drink too much. If I set aside one day a week (or one day a month) to let myself have those pleasures, it may make it easier to then limit myself on the other days."

If we recognize that we are falling into a habit of hours of cable news consumption per evening after work, maybe we can actively schedule time with friends to distract us from this habit. We might even make a commitment to cut our cable television service and opt for other forms of information instead. We can alter our availability to technology and all of the information that goes along with it by designating only certain hours of the day where we are available for texting or social media. We can also monitor our screen time and set boundaries for the amount of time (and attention) we are devoting to our phones and other devices. As Hershfield says, "There are countless apps and programs that can allow us to quantify our behaviors, categorize our actions, and see where we have progressed and/or where we have failed. The upshot is that we have a much clearer picture of exactly the ways in which we succumb to instant gratification, and can therefore see where we can improve." Through this analysis, we can see the time, and perhaps most importantly the attention, we have devoted to items and experiences that are inconsistent with our long-term goals. Given that the emotional parts of our brain tend to fuel instant gratification, we can associate emotions with some of our long-term goals as well. We can consider the excitement of losing that weight before the holidays, looking trimmer and healthier for friends and family, or perhaps identify the specific tangible benefits to our career of working those extra hours on a project at work. Conversely, we can take some of the emotion away from the things that bring us instant gratification, reflecting upon the returns that we see in our investment of both time and attention. We may find that those impulses are not serving us well, and we can alter our environment to avoid them. It is when the repeated behaviors start to keep us from our best lives that we run into trouble. We can keep our eye on the long-term, while along the way reward ourselves in the short-term with little prizes that keep us on track towards that bigger goal. As for that bakery on the way home from my run, perhaps I will take the long way home and celebrate my achievement with the bathroom scale in the morning!

CHAPTER 15

Loneliness

Amy has over 1,000 friends on Facebook. She admits that she used to spend "a few hours a day" scrolling through her newsfeed, posting pictures, and commenting on the postings of other friends. She says that of the 1,000 people on Facebook, she thinks she "probably knew" about 10% of them but even many of those are people who were classmates from high school or college from decades ago. "If I had a free moment or if I was dealing with something difficult, I would just scroll through to see what was up. Sometimes, like during the elections a few years ago, I think I was logging on to find a reason to get ticked off about something from the other party." In 2018, Amy began to realize that she wasn't happy with her social life, thinking that she didn't have a close circle of friends that she could confide in or who could confide in her. "I just realized that I had no one in my life who really knew me. My family is far away and my connections were on social media. It is tough to say it, but I was lonely. I had no one. I look back on it now and say to myself, 'You were on Facebook or texting with someone when you could have been volunteering or joining a group or something where you could meet people in-person, not just some profile' . . . I wasted a lot of time. The couple hours a day on Facebook added up and it took away from making some real connections. I look back on that time now and think that I almost wasted it." Amy has deleted her Facebook app and only logs in via her laptop but just to "check in" once in a while. She is volunteering in a local mentorship program and joined a few clubs for people in their 30s and 40s to try to connect with other people. "It's better now. I don't have a million close personal friends so I am still working on it, but at least what I am doing is real and not just sitting and looking at other people's stuff on my phone all day."

Loneliness is "the emotional distress that results when inherent needs for intimacy and companionship are not met." Loneliness has become widespread. In a recent survey of over 10,000 adults, Cigna found that 61% of respondents stated that they were lonely. In 2018, the UK prime minister established a loneliness strategy that would help the estimated nine million people there who go sometimes weeks and even months without human contact. This loneliness strategy also included the new position of Minister of Loneliness. As the *Economist* wrote in 2018, "Loneliness is the leprosy of the 21st century, eating away at its victims and repelling those who encounter it." Loneliness is subjective, so no matter how many friends or close family you may have around you, you could still have that feeling. A whopping 60% of married couples identify as lonely. In many cases, loneliness is the lack of a deep connection with one or more individuals, where each individual is openly sharing with the other. We see that the lack of connection expands even to the workplace. The same Cigna research suggested that those who had meaningful connections at work were less likely to be lonely. What is most striking is that those who were new to their positions scored six points higher in the loneliness scale than those who had been working in their current jobs for 10 years or more.

It is important to note that there is a difference between solitude and loneliness. One can be lonely while in the presence of other people. Think of people who are in relationships who may feel some sense of loneliness. Some individuals who are around others throughout most of their personal and professional lives are still lonely. Loneliness has been linked to higher risks for a number of physical and psychological conditions, including heart disease, depression, and cognitive decline. In fact, in the same report, Cigna suggested that loneliness had the same health effects as smoking 15 cigarettes per day! Solitude, on the other hand, is about being with yourself and disconnecting with the outside world in many ways, usually creating a space for reflection and contemplation. Individuals can be in a state of solitude and not be the least bit lonely.

There are three types of loneliness. First, existential loneliness relates to our feelings of being alone as a human, where we come into the world alone and leave it alone as well. The feelings of existential loneliness can occur even if you are in a healthy relationship or surrounded by a close group of friends. However, experiencing existential loneliness can be a healthy exercise, as it helps us better address the meaning and purpose of our lives and potentially embark on a spiritual journey or find new purpose in some way, shape, or form. Emotional loneliness relates to the feeling that you lack close relationships, usually someone to confide in. It can also relate to the feeling that you are the only one not in a romantic relationship of some sort. Psychologists suggest that there are no "quick fixes" for this feeling, but certainly making an effort to engage with new people and groups can help to build closer relationships with others. Finally, social loneliness relates to the feeling that one is not part of a larger group of some sort. Regardless of whether one is in a romantic relationship, feelings of social loneliness can occur if one is not accepted into a larger circle of friends or people with whom you share a common bond of some sort. Volunteering or participating in some community function, even connecting with the staff at your favorite restaurant or bar, can be helpful. When we feel lonely, brain regions associated with distress and rumination are activated. People who experience loneliness tend to be more negative and question the intentions of others and, in some cases, experience anxiety. Matthews and a team of neuroscientists discovered that neurons in a region of the brain called the dorsal raphe nucleus were activated when there was some element of social isolation, creating motivation to search for new social connections. In essence, it shows that we need some element of social interaction in our lives and perhaps crave it from a neurological perspective.

Loneliness with 750 of Your Closest Facebook Friends

When it comes to loneliness in this information age, there are clearly mixed benefits. Technology enables us to connect and communicate with others who are both close and far. We can keep up with friends and family who are geographically dispersed and feel like we have a sense of what is occurring in their lives. William Chopik examined the benefits of technology as it relates to loneliness and other health conditions among 600 older adults who used smartphones, including email, social media, video/phone calls, and chatting/ instant messaging. He found that those who used these forms of social technology had lower levels of loneliness and better overall health, including fewer instances of depression.

In many cases, technology can be a powerful tool in strengthening existing relationships. Through the COVID-19 pandemic, technology was incredibly valuable in substituting for in-person connections, which were not possible during the quarantine. Through Zoom, Skype, instant messaging, and clever ways to participate in virtual movie nights where people would stream movies at the same time and chat about them on a number of social media platforms, technology bridged the gap and brought people together who otherwise would not be able to engage. Pandemic or not, people who are unable to physically engage others due to age or health reasons or are geographically isolated can find ways to connect digitally. As discussed earlier, social media platforms such as Facebook and Instagram are valuable tools to strengthen existing relationships with family and friends.

At the same time, technology can also create barriers to in-person connections. "Phubbing" is defined as the act of ignoring someone you are with and giving attention to your cell phone instead. We have all done it and have had it done to us. What is somewhat surprising is that phubbing is bad for both the "phubber" and the "phubbee." A study of 243 married Chinese adults found that phubbing contributed to lower relationship satisfaction and even to depression. The pitfalls of putting a higher priority on your phone than your partner seems to be rather intuitive as your attention is with someone or something else, whether an email, text, or social media. At the same time, researchers in British Columbia found that of the 300 people who participated in the study, those who engaged their phones during dinner had a significant decrease in their overall enjoyment and dining experience. Incidentally, the same researchers conducted a second study of 100 individuals, texting them five times throughout the day for a week, engaging them about their emotional state as well as what they were doing. They found that those who were having face-to-face interaction with other people were far happier than those who were engaged on their phones. The focus on our screens can certainly come at a cost if we are substituting quality time with those closest to us for a digital engagement of some sort.

Loneliness

We have outlined many of the challenges related to social media and loneliness in previous chapters. Of individuals who self-described as heavy social media users, 73% identified as lonely, whereas 52% of light social media users identified as lonely. It is unclear if it is a "chicken-or-egg" notion, meaning are lonely people inherently drawn to social media or does social media make people feel lonelier? However, it does seem clear that many turn to social media thinking it can be a substitute for a more genuine in-person connection. As Catherine Steiner-Adair, author of *The Big Disconnect: Protecting Childhood and Family Relationships in the Digital Age*, states, "There is a confusion between your face-timing or texting and real intimacy. We are hardwired as a species for visceral attachment and connection and trying to achieve that through some online engagement tends to leave us wanting more." Nothing matches the genuine connection of being with another human being and seeing their facial reactions, vocal inflection, or even human touch. Without it, as she states, we continue to search for it. "Electronic engagement is kind of like when a fat-free or healthy version of a cookie is introduced. People are so excited thinking they are going to have the same experience as with the high fat treat, but in reality, without the sugar and fat, it isn't the same. People tend to binge on the healthy version because they crave the dopamine fix, but the fat-free version doesn't give it to them . . . as it's the fat on our palette that gives us the dopamine hit. It is the same with social media, people are hungry for connection and then end up binging on social media that again, doesn't give them what they are craving in authentic human interaction." Given that our time and attention are both scarce commodities, binging on social media can come at the expense of creating and cultivating authentic connections with others.

Yang explored the relationship between Instagram use and loneliness. Through a survey of 208 undergraduate participants, he found that activities related to interaction and browsing on Instagram were both related to lower levels of loneliness. Contrarily, those Instagram users who broadcast, regularly posting pictures, were associated with higher levels of loneliness. As Yang points out, those users who interact and scroll are more likely to keep in touch with friends through Instagram as well as bring users' attention to different friends and contacts they may have. Those who broadcast regularly may indirectly be looking for some element of support from their contacts or, at a minimum, be looking for attention since they may feel lonely and isolated. Of course, it is still unclear whether Instagram (or any social media platform, for that matter) makes people more or less lonely. As discussed in previous chapters, it does appear that those who use social media platforms to connect with existing contacts are likely to be less lonely and are potentially using the platform as a tool for more genuine, in-person experiences. There also may be opportunity costs for those who spend considerable time posting, taking the time to take curated selfies to potentially attract attention from other users. All of this effort to attract and promote on social media may come at the expense of searching for more authentic interactions with others.

The distraction that social media, and our phones in general, cause in our lives could also impact our interpersonal connections. The feeling of distraction and lowered enjoyment of an experience could potentially be transmitted across our social calendars where at least a portion of our attention is devoted to our phones at the expense of being present with humans who are with us. If our attention is even partly devoted to our likes on social media or a text message we are expecting, that can limit our ability to fully engage in the experience in which we are currently occupied. Essentially, who wants to spend time with someone who is phubbing them constantly? It is important to note that it isn't that people who have their phones with them all of the time are all lonely. However, if we are not fully engaged in our experiences with other people, over time it may limit us in being our full selves to others and limit what we perceive as enjoyment in the company of other people.

The multitude of connections that each of us have on social media, as well as the countless ways we engage other people via technology, can create an expectation of constant connection. There is an expectation that we will receive that text or instant message and when it does not arrive quickly, some struggle. The threshold by which we are able to handle any form of short-term isolation seems to be much lower than it was in our grandparents' day. There certainly was no social media at that time, nor was there texting. People likely felt real feelings of loneliness then, but perhaps the difference was the level of expectation that previous generations had when it came to engagement compared to us in this information age. We expect to get that text, that digital engagement of some sort. And when it does not come, it causes feelings of neglect and potentially anxiety. There is also an added element of FOMO here, where social media plays a role in the expectations we have for experiences in our lives. As former U.S. Surgeon General Vivek Murthy writes in his book, *Together,* "The irony is that our capacity for solitude is also diminished by technology. Social media's constant presence creates the illusion that we never need to be alone and that something must be wrong with us if we *feel alone.* Yet we still need solitude, as well as the time and the space to cultivate its benefits. We need regularly to free our minds to wander and explore without being directed by network algorithms and autoplay ads. Solitude allows us to get comfortable being with ourselves, which makes it easier to *be* ourselves in interactions with others. That authenticity helps build strong connections."

There are many ways in which we can address loneliness in our lives. We can use our feelings of existential loneliness as a license to live life to the fullest, making the most of all of the experiences that life has to offer. We can be proactive in engaging people to develop deeper friendships, rather than waiting for others to contact us. Participation in groups that are larger than ourselves can be a powerful way to experience a sense of belonging and empowerment. It could be as simple as being more active in the community through volunteering or even just joining our local gym. Through all of those experiences, being thoughtful about our digital engagement can potentially open us up to engaging others. In other words, it is tough to meet people and make friends if we are constantly buried in our phones all the time. Whether as single people or as couples, we all need to feel as if we have a footprint that we are somehow impacting, even if it is just through positive interactions with those in our community.

Steiner-Adair suggests that we all have the opportunity to consider the amount of time we are spending on our smartphones or the web and be proactive about ensuring that social media and similar platforms are working for us. "We should reflect upon both our in-person and digital experiences and if there is too much time online or on our phones, we should take charge of it. Maybe we make a schedule of how much time we engage it all. The reality is that if you don't take charge of it, it will hijack your social life." She suggests finding ways to engage beyond social media and our phones, because the avenue that we use to communicate with others can have a profound impact on the strength and quality of our relationships. Even as couples, only sending texts that discuss the chores or events of the day can weaken relationships and create elements of loneliness.

As Steiner-Adair says, "Texting is so transactional in nature . . . 'pickup the kids, dry cleaning, whatever.' Talking instead of texting can have a huge impact and create a new and better level of intimacy."

Texting or instant messaging can have the same impact throughout our social circle. Picking up the phone or, better yet, meeting in person can facilitate deeper conversations and a better sense of connection. We can feel empowered to make new connections and deepen existing ones. Technology, like social media, is not a destination in itself but a tool to get us there. Once empowered, we have to be purposeful in finding ways to engage. So the next time the chair next to you is open and someone asks, "Is anyone sitting here?" I hope you will say, "No. Please join me." And if by chance a conversation ensues . . . please, no phubbing.

CHAPTER 16

Choice

Think about all the decisions we make in one day. Some of them are thrust upon us as part of modern life and others we actively seek for one reason or another. The number of choices that we encounter is staggering, from work, to food, to our social lives, to how many olives we prefer in our martini. Just with regard to the food we consume, we make over 200 decisions per day, deciding upon not just what we eat, but where we eat, when we eat, and how we eat it. How many times have you stared at a menu while a "patient" waiter offered, "Do you need more time?" Even a menu can be overwhelming, yet whether it is cars, mattresses, or vacation destinations, we like to have as many options as possible. Starbucks advertises that there are 80,000 combinations of drinks to choose from. This clearly relates to all of the different combinations of preferences for each drink, such as no foam, lots of foam, extra hot, not too hot, room for cream, no room for cream, and so on. If you tried one of these combinations daily, it would take you around 200 years to sample each of them. If you found the perfect one in year 83, would you remember that it was perfect 117 years later? I will go out on a limb and say that it is unlikely. Even though we have no use for so many choices, marketers love to showcase them all. Rarely do you hear an ad for hot tubs or tires or whatever where the announcer says, "Come on down! We have limited options for you to choose from!" We want more choices. We inherently feel that if we have more choices, we have a better chance of getting exactly what we want – even if we really have no idea what we want in the first place.

Freedom of choice is one of the hallmarks of a free society. We equate choice with control. We see this as a form of capitalism as we thrive on the power of deciding where we live and what we drive. Choice also has political connotations as well, whether related to reproductive rights, healthcare, or the wearing of masks during a pandemic. Choice and control go hand in hand and can impact our overall well-being in significant ways. In exploring the impact of choice on the health outcomes of seniors in a nursing home, half of the participants in a study was told that they had the choice over how to arrange their furniture and where to socialize and watch movies, whereas the other half was told that the staff had the responsibility to make them happy and limited their choices. Those who were given more freedom of choice were happier and more engaged with other residents than the group who had limited options. A follow-up study by the same researchers found that the group that was given a higher sense of control had a 50% lower mortality rate over the next 18 months than those who had limited control. We have evolved to where our survival instincts encourage us to have more choices, which will – whether rationally or not – make us feel in control of our ultimate outcome. Researchers at the London Business School found that choice and power are two interrelated items. If individuals do not feel a sense of power over their situation, they want more choice. However, if people have more choices, they tend not to strive for more power. There are many elements in our personal and professional lives where we have little control. We are therefore drawn towards areas where we can have more choices.

I Want to Consider All of My Options First

Nobel Prize–winning economist Herbert Simon coined the term "satisficing," which is a combination of the words "satisfy" and "suffice." In his theory of bounded rationality, Simon suggested that individuals do not seek to discover maximum benefit from a course of action. It is impossible to collect and comprehend all of the possible information necessary to make a decision. Satisficers have an internal threshold by which they make a decision, comparing available options to their needs and objectives. Once they discover an option that meets those needs and objectives, they select it. So essentially, satisficers make a decision based upon what is "good enough." Maximizers, on the other hand, feel compelled to evaluate each and every possible option before deciding. It is usually impossible to comprehend all the possible options, let alone collect all the information, before making a decision. Maximizers also tend to experience more regret regarding their choices than satisficers. As more choices become available, the standards by which a maximizer views an option as acceptable tends to increase as well. It is important to note that just because a satisficer makes a decision based upon what she believes is good enough, it does not mean that her standards are necessarily low. She could have very high standards but will make a choice based upon what meets her criteria and not perform an exhaustive search of every possible option. In many cases, we are both maximizers and satisficers. I am a maximizer when it comes to the optimal vacation hotel. I want to search each and every option to find the best location before deciding. However, when it comes to selecting a dishwasher, I am comfortable selecting one that is rated high and within the budget. I do not need to explore all of my options before making a decision.

In likely the most famous study regarding choice, one set of customers at a market was presented with the option of 24 different jams and another set of customers at the same market was presented with just six different jams. Although the larger display with 24 jams garnered more initial interest, customers were 10 times less likely to select a jam with the larger display. Incidentally, those who bought a jar of jam from the choice of six were actually happier with their choice than those who bought from the choice of 24! When we are given more options, it can be difficult to evaluate each different one. It requires more time and cognitive effort. It also can lead to anxiety and worry about making an incorrect decision. More choice may cause us to reflect constantly upon the other options that were available to us. "I knew I should have selected the jam in the second row. Why didn't I do that?!" Unlike situations when there are fewer options, more options make us second-guess the choice we made.

The idea of choice overload spans centuries and has been discussed by philosophers as early as Aristotle. In the fourteenth century, a concept known as Buridan's ass, named after the French philosopher Jean Buridan, depicted a hungry and thirsty donkey placed precisely equidistant between a pile of hay and a pail of water. In the paradox, the donkey dies because it cannot decide between the two options; it is incapacitated by the two choices. Imagine if that poor donkey had to decide upon 30 different brands of hay (including organic); the poor animal wouldn't stand a chance in modern times either!

Choice overload occurs when an individual is overwhelmed by what appears to be similar options. We have difficulty making a decision as we consider potential outcomes as well as the risks associated with making an incorrect choice. A great deal of attention and energy is devoted to weighing the many aspects of each decision. Let's go back to the dinner menu for a moment. As the waiter stares at you, you could be thinking about the taste of each option but also the number of calories, the cost, the perception of eating a particular dish (if you were craving veal maybe), as well as a host of other factors. It can be exhausting, and in some cases paralyzing. Too many options can make it difficult for our brains to process all of the information, evaluate it, and ultimately develop some sort of comparison. Think about how many times you have gone onto a website or into a store with the purpose of purchasing something and ended up deciding upon nothing because there were too many options. An inverted U model can best describe our ideal number of choices. Having no choices is not adequate for us, so as we progress up the U, we see our level of happiness with these choices increase. Our happiness descends as we have too many choices to consider that creates some of this anxiety and paralysis.

Barry Shwartz, author of *The Paradox of Choice*, and his colleagues developed the Maximization Scale to determine individuals' tendency to maximize. You can rate yourself on a scale of 1 to 7, from "completely disagree" to "completely agree."

1. Whenever I'm faced with a choice, I try to imagine what all the other possibilities are, even ones that aren't present at the moment.
2. No matter how satisfied I am with my job, it's only right for me to be on the lookout for better opportunities.
3. When I am in the car listening to the radio, I often check other stations to see if something better is playing, even if I am relatively satisfied with what I'm listening to.

4. When I watch TV, I channel surf, often scanning through the available options even while attempting to watch one program.
5. I treat relationships like clothing: I expect to try a lot on before finding the perfect fit.
6. I often find it difficult to shop for a gift for a friend.
7. Renting videos is really difficult. I'm always struggling to pick the best one.
8. When shopping, I have a hard time finding clothing that I really love.
9. I'm a big fan of lists that attempt to rank things (the best movies, the best singers, the best athletes, the best novels, etc.).
10. I find that writing is very difficult, even if it's just writing a letter to a friend, because it's so hard to word things just right. I often do several drafts of even simple things.
11. No matter what I do, I have the highest standards for myself.
12. I never settle for second best.
13. I often fantasize about living in ways that are quite different from my actual life.

How did you score? As Schwartz states, the people whose average rating is four and above tend to be maximizers. Kristi Hedges, executive coach and author of *The Inspiration Code*, states, "The old saying about perfect being the enemy of the good applies. We need to think about what is good enough for us and realize that the mental energy to make all of these choices does not, or usually does not, equate to the importance of the decision. Focusing on what we need and will satisfy whatever need we have at that time is a better approach." In reality, there is an element of mental energy for the maximizer both during the process of choosing in first collecting all of the information, as well as afterwards, as the maximizer considers and reconsiders what could have been with a different decision.

The information age brings with it a seemingly unlimited number of choices for us in our daily lives. Exhibit A would be Amazon, where we have access to mountains of brands and types of almost anything. Amazon could be a maximizers' delight. You can spend all day exploring each brand and type of running sock, comparing prices, colors, and the ability to repel moisture, and of course, reading the reviews. This person said that running sock A is the best, but she also mentioned that when she was wearing those socks, she was not actually running. Another person liked a different sock, is an avid runner, but had difficulty with the sock when they had poor running shoes. What do you do at that point? It can be an all-day experience!

As we discussed in Chapter 7, we see the same issue with online dating. We can be as specific as we want in determining the height, weight, hair color, and a host of other variables in finding a perfect mate. As with Amazon, this can seem overwhelming as well, even though there are no user reviews on Tinder like there are for Amazon. (One can only imagine how those would read!) Nevertheless, a maximizer can be overwhelmed with online dating, searching through each possible option before finally deciding on a potential mate. There is also a higher likelihood that the maximizer might feel regret about their choice of a new mate. Perhaps a good first question to a potential mate when chatting on an online dating platform is whether the person is a maximizer or a satisficer.

The information age also gives us the ability to research any potential choice via technology. We have at our disposal a mountain of information that we can reference when deciding upon a college, automobile, or new neighborhood to live in. Each and every person who has made similar choices to ours has the ability to post their own experience with that decision, which can help us be better informed. The challenge of this mountain of information is that everyone – and I do mean everyone – can post their opinion. Many of those opinions are biased and uninformed. As Schwartz says in *The Paradox of Choice*, "The avalanche of electronic information we now face is such that in order to solve the problem of choosing from 200 brands of cereal or 5,000 mutual funds, we must first solve the problem of choosing from 10,000 websites offering to make us more informed consumers." In order to make an informed choice, we have to sift through information from a variety of both reputable and not-so-reputable sources to determine what is reliable.

Not only does technology provide accessibility to more choices and information regarding those choices, but it can also make us question our past choices. Social media in particular can be a continuous reminder of our past choices. A maximizer who is logged into Facebook and is impacted by the pictures of perfect frolicking families might question many of her life choices and maybe even experience anxiety over some of those choices. The daily reminder, whether fictional or not, that the maximizers' decisions do not appear to be the very best choice can take a toll. Chou and Edge found that the more time people spent on Facebook, the more they felt that life was unfair and that other people had better lives. As we discussed earlier, this unfair comparison can be more likely when participants were following contacts on social media whom they did not know personally. When we have real-life interactions with others, we hear about their successes in their jobs and relationships, but we also hear about their challenges. Many of the challenges that a friend would share with us over a coffee are not things that people would post on Facebook. Through sustained engagement on social media, the choices that we make in almost every aspect of our lives are now under a microscope and scrutinized . . . by us. In many cases, those choices are in comparison to the choices we think were made by others.

Combating Choice Overload

Hedges suggests that there are three things we can do to help with choice overload. First, we can put some parameters around the amount of time we are willing to spend on making a decision. "Decide that you are going to spend a day or a week on something and give yourself that time to collect enough information to make a choice and then make it." There are choices where the search process in the role of a maximizer is fun, where you enjoy searching each and every option. People who love cars may take months to learn about different brands, test-drive them, and talk with friends and neighbors about possible options because it is a fun journey, particularly if you have someone else to share in it with you. Those processes are encouraged. However, if you have to select something a bit more mundane, you can create a timeframe for how much time and energy you will devote to the process and stick to it. For example, you might say that by the end of the month, you will make a decision regarding your next apartment. In that scenario, you have all week to develop a budget, explore options, look at properties, and maybe even talk with friends about the options. Once the end of the week arrives, it is time to decide.

Second, Hedges suggests that our intuition can be a powerful tool in helping us make good decisions. "Our bodies can tell us things that our minds sometimes do not want to hear. Let the decision marinate over a certain amount of time, follow your gut, and ultimately make a decision." Finally, she advises to be aware of the all-or-nothing type of thinking. For example, if you're considering taking a new job, you may become overwhelmed with the potential consequences of a career move and start thinking about small things, like the new commute, to hypothetical scenarios like "Will I get along with my new boss?" or "What happens if the company where my new job is located goes bankrupt?" As Hedges states, "The reality is that none of these items are unchangeable. You make the decision and regardless of the outcome, you observe, you change, and you learn from it." Even after a decision was made that led to a potentially negative outcome, she emphasizes the importance of reminding ourselves that we can only make decisions based upon the information that we have at a given time. We should forgive ourselves and not belabor past decisions. All of us can certainly learn from past decisions but not blame ourselves for deciding based upon what we thought was a good course of action. As she states, "turn everything into a learning opportunity. If you took a job and didn't like it, it is valuable information for us going forward."

Finding credible sources to help make decisions can be invaluable. Product reviews from users and social media are great ways to learn more about the journey of others who made a similar choice, but it comes with challenges. In our process of making choices, we essentially have to make choices about the sources of information we can trust, which will ultimately help us make our choice! This requires extra vigilance on our part to determine who and what can provide us with good information, which could include trusted friends, websites that offer unbiased and uncompensated reviews, and data from reliable sources. Whether we are a satisficer or a maximizer, choices can be tough, but they can be a lot easier if we are as well-informed as possible. Even the waiter brings his own bias to a menu recommendation. So as the waiter is still standing there patiently awaiting your selection, maybe you realize that the time has come to make a decision, go with your gut, and select the chicken. If it doesn't work out, you will learn from the experience and choose better next time. Besides, you can always make up for your poor choice of entrée when it comes time for dessert.

CHAPTER 17

Impulse Buying

Every summer, my family would take our annual trip to Cedar Point, a large amusement park in Ohio. We would set up camp there for the weekend and ride as many of the roller coasters as possible. One year, my parents gave my sister and me a sum of money to spend in the park. "Don't spend it all in one place," was the quote we heard as Dad handed us a few twenties before the trip. Once in the park, I would not stop thinking about where I would spend this money (there was zero chance that any cash was going back home with me). I walked the park with this money – not in pocket, but in hand – thinking about hats, T-shirts, and what value this cash would bring me at the arcade. The choices were overwhelming; I deliberated almost the entire trip and eventually settled for some cotton candy and a stack of useless tickets that represented my triumphs at Skee-Ball. All that I had to show for this money was progress towards a few cavities and a Teenage Mutant Ninja Turtles pencil sharpener. Today, the sharpener is nowhere to be found . . . and of course, neither is the cash. Whether we're children or adults, sometimes knowing the best place to spend our money is difficult. As Andy Rooney once said, "We are good at earning money. We just don't know what to do with it once we have it." I don't know if I earned that money during that trip to the amusement park or not, but looking back, I would certainly agree with Andy that I did not know what to do with it once I got it.

Financial decision-making, at its core, examines our decisions as they relate to money. Those decisions focus on how we spend, save, and invest. Usually, our 401(k) and savings accounts are good indicators of the types of decisions we make when it comes to money. Maximizing our 401(k) contribution is a good indicator of our strong interest, and perhaps ability, to invest our earnings towards long-term goals. If we have a budget, there is only a finite amount of cash at our disposal in a month or maybe even in a given day. Putting aside the many ways we can rack up personal debt, the amount we spend should be equal to (or hopefully less than) what we are earning. We also have to be forward-thinking in exploring not only our current expenses but also how they might change in the future. We think about potential changes to our income as well as how all of this might impact our retirement plans and paying for our children's education. As if our financial decisions were not difficult enough, retailers work to maximize impulse buying, luring us into spending money on items that we do not need (or do not need so much of). Look no further than the candy at the grocery store checkout lines, and of course the compelling headlines in the tabloids. Amazon and online retailers of all kinds also make suggestions that lure us into spending more than what we originally intended.

On average, consumers spend $5,400 per year on impulse purchases, which range from chocolate to clothes to, in some cases, cars. Impulse buying occurs for a number of reasons, most notably because there is some emotional component to the purchase. There is a pure pleasure that comes from buying something on a whim during what is typically a boring trip to the store or a routine purchase online. It can make us feel good in the moment, maybe because it is delicious candy or because we think we look good in it. There is also an element of loss aversion here. Many of us do not want to miss out on something that is going to be good, or because we suspect that the product has limited availability, or that the price may only be discounted for a specific period of time. After the fact, if we reflect on the purchase, we sometimes feel regret because the money we spent could have gone to saving or paying down debt. Three out of four Americans make impulse purchases of some kind, with over half who do saying they experience some sort of buyer's remorse. Yet some of us just keep doing it.

Fighting for Our Attention

Similar to our financial decision-making, there are a multitude of places we can spend our attention. In fact, we make far more decisions regarding where to direct our attention than where to spend our money. Think about your day today. You may have started your morning focusing on your sore shoulder after an intense workout the day before. You may have thought that you are just getting older (and haven't worked out in ages). Within seconds, your mind went from your shoulder to the weather report on TV and then to the shirt you were planning to wear to work, while also focusing on someone yelling something downstairs that may or may not be directed at you. You then momentarily thought of the schedule for the day ahead before returning to the situation with the shirt. Oh, and why is someone yelling downstairs?

We are constantly focusing and shifting our attention based upon internal and external factors. At work, you might focus your attention on the body language of your boss during an important meeting, ignoring the content of the discussions (essentially, a one-hour meeting with you ignoring a strategic plan and instead wondering if the boss's body language represents a 2% or 5% raise at the end of the year). And we are constantly distracted. I can attend a concert or a speech and direct my attention solely on the hairstyle or necktie of the person on stage, completely ignoring the content of the performance. Within seconds, we can focus, divide, and redirect our attention to numerous sights and sounds. Sometimes we direct our attention based upon our goals and sometimes we are just plain distracted. Advertisers of all kinds are also competing for our attention. We see ads everywhere, from banner ads on websites and smartphones to television commercials and signs and placards. It is difficult even to use a public restroom without seeing some advertisement of some sort. As mentioned in an earlier chapter, we are living in an attention economy and many people want our attention for one reason or another. We spend our attention on a broad range of people, places, and things, sometimes purposefully and sometimes habitually.

Added to all of that competition for our attention is technology. As I have already outlined, the collection of functions and apps on our smartphones are all designed to lure our attention to them. Beyond just advertisements, the web is designed for us to surf from site to site, starting with looking up a basic fact and then, next thing you know, it is 45 minutes later and we are Googling our high school boyfriend as our fact-finding mission has now evolved into a "where are they now" festival starring people you have not interacted with in years and co-starring a lot of wasted time. As we will discuss later in further detail, most of the apps on our phones are designed for us to be the product and not the user, keeping us engaged both to maximize advertising revenue as well as compile copious amounts of personal data.

With the average amount of time on smartphones over four hours per day, one cannot help but think that this time engaged with our phones is getting in the way of larger life goals and our important relationships. Think about our spending power relative to attention. If we are spending our attention on technology, it is at the expense of other activities. Returning to the analogy of financial decision-making, you can think of these frequent, habitual visits to our smartphones like an impulse buy. Each of us "spends" our attention on these platforms at varying levels, but it is utilizing a scarce resource towards an activity that may not be serving our long-term or even short-term interests. It is not that devoting even some attention towards social media or other technology platforms is a horrible thing – no different than it is not the worst thing in the world to treat yourself to a candy bar for a job well done or a good workout. The issue with both our financial spending and how we spend our attention is solely a matter of what each of us can afford.

If we want to have control of our life, we need to have control of our attention. We have to be intentional about what is most important to us to avoid being reactive to the sights and sounds that come from modern life. In his book, *Stand Out of Our Light,* James Williams offers the distinction between pettiness and prudence when it comes to the relationship between distraction and short- and long-term goals. Pettiness, as he defines it, is pursuit of a short-term goal as if it had a higher intrinsic value than it actually does. Pettiness can include posting on social media or spending time forwarding emails regarding all kinds of minor topics to contacts. The short-term goal is attention from those on social media or the people we are forwarding clever (and not so clever) emails. The short-term goal can also be that dopamine hit that comes from engaging social media or the seeking of new and relevant or not-so-relevant information. Prudence, as expected, is the abstaining from present pleasure to focus on longer-term or greater pleasure in the future. Everyone decides the goals of their lives on their own and we all are different. Some people want to have the most impactful career possible. Others value family ahead of their career. There are a million other short- and long-term goals that each of us are pursuing, all of which are different but equally important. However, when it comes to our attention decision-making, days, weeks, months, and years of pettiness can be strung together, where a constant pursuit of social media attention leads to a place that is not within our long-term vision of ourselves or our loved ones. One impulse buy of our attention will not derail the future we envision, but an impulse buy for hours each day over the course of months and years can be problematic.

Self-regulation is acting through your behaviors, thoughts, and emotions in accordance with your long-term best interests. Self-regulation comes from within, as we attempt either to meet a personal goal or to maintain a current status of something in our lives. Whether we're talking about belonging to a group or meeting individual personal goals, self-regulation can be quite helpful in many aspects of our lives. It might be thinking about the money you save while resisting the urge to buy that shirt just because it is on sale. Perhaps it is thinking twice about that piece of chocolate cake. With our attention, self-regulation could be considering the long-term benefits of finishing a major project at work rather than focusing on our newsfeed on social media. We might consider the implications on the relationships around us when we spend hours a day on our smartphones. Essentially, self-regulation is really thinking before you act, considering the longer term rather than the short-term reward. Even while engaged in information and technology, self-regulation could help us in limiting the effects of some of the negative emotions of sensationalism in news or even engaging in debate with strangers via social media. Tim Pychyl, author of *Solving the Procrastination Puzzle: A Concise Guide to Strategies for Change,* views self-regulation similar to a thermostat, which sets a standard and then monitors and tracks the temperature to meet that standard. However, he adds that our problems are typically not captured by this simplistic model. "Many people falsely view self-regulation as *under*-regulation where if we are not meeting our goals, we are not working hard enough, or have not created high enough standards for ourselves in some area. In reality, it is *mis*-regulation, where we carry some false belief about what will make us feel better." We think that eating those cookies, or spending an extra hour going down a rabbit hole on YouTube or Twitter will make us feel better.

In the short term, it might (notwithstanding the guilt we often feel). However, in the long term, we recognize the self-defeating nature, even irrationality of our choices, feeling a fair amount of self-loathing about not acting in our long-term interests or missing out on something important to us for some short-term reward.

Creating an Attention Budget

In his 2015 *New York Times* article, Carl Richards states, "Pretend you woke up tomorrow morning and someone took all of the things you now pay for with attention and switched it to money. To spend time on Facebook, you would have to enter your credit card number. To check out what your friends are doing on Instagram, you would need to pull out that card again. How much time would you spend on Twitter then?" If we can think about attention as not only a finite resource, but also something tangible, then we may find ourselves being more responsible with it. We might even begin to track our attention spending! Our focused attention can lead to stronger relationships with those we love, more effective careers, and perhaps a stronger sense of faith and self. It does not happen magically, but if we want to have better relationships and careers, we have to focus on them. Similarly, if our life's dream is to be the best Fortnite player ever, we have to devote time and attention to playing it. Therefore, recognition that our attention is not only finite, but also of incredible value in helping us do the things that are most important to us, could be useful. Asking ourselves, "Did I use my attention today in a way that will make me happy?" could help us in our future decisions.

Any expert who advises individuals regarding their budget will tell you that the key components of monitoring your spending are, first, to create a budget outlining what you need to spend in a given period of time. These are everything from life's necessities to the vacation that you are planning for next year. Second, monitor and document all of your spending. This tracks your behavior to see where your money is actually going to determine if it is within your budget. There is then a focus on where funds are being invested, whether in retirement or on the house or family. With money, we all have at least some sense of the value of it as it relates to our living expenses and perhaps even our long-term future. The value of attention, on the other hand, is a bit more difficult for some people to understand and quantify. If we can begin to see the value of it, we then may be inclined to think more critically about where we want to spend it. Similar to cash, we can also invest our attention in long-term goals such as our education, careers, or strengthening our relationships with those around us. Thoughtless spending habits with both our money and our attention have similar long-term impacts on our lives. With our bank and investment accounts, there is a number that represents those decisions and impulses, whereas with attention, it is much more difficult to quantify, but the effects can be just as powerful.

Similar to procrastination, the management of our attention needs to move away from our emotions and towards action. As Pychyl says, "With procrastination, your attention is focused on emotions. We can also focus our attention away from our emotions and towards our actions. Most people think it is a time management problem, but procrastination is actually an emotion-management problem." We tend to give into our emotions, just like the old saying, "If it feels good, do it." With our attention, Pychyl suggests that we curb the "amygdala hijack," which is the point where our emotional "reptile" brain dominates the executive, rational processing of our prefrontal cortex. "We need to move our attention away from our emotions and towards an action. Many people say motivation drives action, but in reality, action drives motivation. If we can find the lowest threshold action to begin our process of self-regulation, we can be motivated to take further action." In terms of self-regulating our attention, it might be moving our smartphones to another room or limiting the time that we are available to text or watch the news. Metacognitive skills, such as reflection and, even better, meditation, can help us evaluate and become more aware of our actions. As Pychyl states, "It is a non-judgmental awareness of our actions and emotions, acknowledging those feelings without being those feelings. For example, I can *have* fear without *being* my fear."

Just because we have money in our hand doesn't mean we have to spend it. We can think about how that money could help us during a rainy day or invest it as we think about our future. Perhaps more valuable than our money, our attention is a resource that requires thoughtful consideration regarding where we spend it. Similar to money, there are many places where we can easily waste our attention for some sort of short-term gain at the expense of authentic experiences, personal relationships, and long-term goals. We do not have to passively accept the many places where our attention can be wasted relative to our personal and professional goals. We can actively monitor where we spend our attention and if it is not serving us, we can alter it. If we constantly reflect upon where we are spending our attention and self-regulate, we can make better use of this valuable resource. Just like that kid at the amusement park who spent that handful of cash, we don't want to look back on any experience wondering why we spent our attention in places that might have reacted to a short-term emotion but didn't necessarily make us happy. Our attention is a valuable resource. Spend wisely!

CHAPTER 18

Porn

Pornography is much older than the internet. In fact, one can make the argument that it stretches back thousands of years. The Venus of Willendorf, developed around 28,000 BCE, is a four-inch-tall statue of a rather voluptuous woman and identified as the first artifact of pornography. Depictions of nudity and sexual acts continued across cultures and centuries after, including Babylon and ancient Greece. During the Middle Ages, pornographic literature was popular even though it was not looked upon kindly by the church. The literature included both drawings and text that was designed exclusively for the sexual pleasure of its readers. The first pornographic movie was made in the 1880s, coinciding with some of the first films ever made. Pornography during that time usually consisted of people walking around their homes naked and not necessarily performing any type of sexual act. Well into the twentieth century, films became more and more popular, depicting sex acts of all kinds. The 1970s saw a birth of multiple companies that produced porn, depicting both heterosexual and homosexual acts. With the dawn of the internet in the 1990s, pornography became easy to access and usually free of charge.

Pornography is defined as "printed or visual material containing the explicit description or display of sexual organs or activity, intended to stimulate erotic rather than aesthetic or emotional feelings." We all have different thresholds for what we think is pornographic or obscene. Even the government has challenges in defining some of the content, with the most famous incident beginning with U.S. Supreme Court Justice Potter Stewart saying, "I know when I see it," referring to his minimum requirements for porn. The porn industry today generates $12 billion dollars a year in revenue, a figure that any one of the major American television networks could only dream of achieving. Data regarding actual porn consumption and demographics is a bit tricky to identify as most online sites do not traditionally release their data. However, Pornhub, the largest online porn site, cites that in 2019, they had 42 billion visits to their site, averaging 115 million site visits per day, "which is the equivalent of the populations of Canada, Australia, Poland, and the Netherlands." And they have lots of videos. In 2019, there were 6.83 million new videos uploaded onto Pornhub. As they put it, "If you strung all of 2019's new video content together and started watching them way back in 1850, you'd still be watching them today!" As Pornhub states, there are 50,000 searches per minute and 800 searches per second, which equates to "the same number of hamburgers that McDonald's sells every second." There is a joke about a happy meal in there somewhere.

Porn Consumption

Clearly a lot of people are watching porn, but who are they? According to Pornhub, the audience breakdown is 75% men and 25% women, with an average age of 36 years old. The peak hours for visits to porn websites are 4–5 p.m. and 10 p.m.–1 a.m., so perhaps right after school and after everyone else, including the partner or spouse, has gone to sleep. The average visit to the Pornhub site is just 10 minutes. Incidentally, two of the days where porn consumption is the lowest are New Year's Day and Super Bowl Sunday. Conservative states tend to have a higher amount of porn consumption where visitors are on the site for longer periods of time.

There are lots of reasons to explain the high demand for porn. We are obviously sexually active creatures with sexual desires. Just a few centuries ago, people married right at puberty. As soon as young adults were of age to procreate, they married and became more sexually active with their partner. Today, given advancements in healthcare and nutrition, puberty occurs much younger and marriage occurs much later, so many of those young adults are likely part of the 4–5 p.m. peak afterschool crowd on some porn sites. For older adults, the burdens of modern life can get in the way of a healthy sexual relationship, whether as a single person or part of a couple or marriage. As David Ludden, professor of psychology at Georgia Gwinnett College says, "Nowadays, we work longer hours and experience far more stress on a daily basis than people did even a century ago. Also, the shift to the nuclear family (as opposed to the extended family) means that the burdens of childcare now fall squarely on the shoulders of the two parents. All these stresses and demands for time are disruptive for relationships, making it more difficult for couples to find the time or the desire for sexual intimacy." Given this disruption, there is a need for an outlet for sexual urges, and porn can provide this outlet.

For single people, porn use can merely be utilitarian outside of a relationship. It can certainly be safer than having multiple partners. It can also be much cheaper in that you do not have to buy dinner or go on a date! There has been a long-held belief that single people who partake in pornography may be less likely to be interested in any type of significant relationship. This theory suggests that men are willing to exchange the elements of a long-term relationship for sexual satisfaction, a form of sexual capital if you will. Samuel Perry explored data sets of single men and found that those who regularly consumed pornography were actually more interested in marriage than those who did not. As Perry states, "This may imply that pornography does not replace the benefits of a committed relationship."

For couples, it is a bit more challenging. As Ludden says, "For other mixed-sex couples, porn use is more problematic. People with conservative sexual attitudes invariably fall into the heterosexual norm, and for them porn is unacceptable. One common pattern goes like this. Both the husband and the wife subscribe to the traditional model whereby the male is the pursuer and the female is the gatekeeper. The husband asks for sex and the wife refuses. While the wife may acquiesce sometimes, she "guards the gate" often enough that the husband loses confidence and stops pursuing altogether. Instead, he masturbates to porn to satisfy his unmet sexual needs. He also feels very guilty about it. When the wife finds out, she's offended

and blames porn as the reason why they aren't having sex anymore."
It is, therefore, not that porn is to blame for the lack of intimacy,
but as Ludden puts it, porn is only the outlet to what is the primary
issue in the relationship. He suggests that this is where a relationship
counselor can play a pivotal role in identifying the primary issue and
not blaming the symptom.

Two researchers from the University of Oklahoma conducted a
longitudinal study of porn use and marriage. Surveying couples over
the course of eight years, they found that the probability of divorce
close to doubled when pornography was somehow introduced into
the relationship between survey waves. The real issue concerns
the "chicken or the egg" paradox. It is possible that unhappy couples were bringing pornography into their lives because they were
unhappy. Perhaps they were unfilled in some way so they turned to
porn. Conversely, it could be that the presence of porn created issues
for the relationship, whether sexual or otherwise. It may be that for
couples, how the porn is viewed is key. Researchers at the University of Arkansas compared the use of pornography among men and
women and found that, in surveying both, men tended to use pornography in a more "utilitarian" way, while women used it as a form
of lovemaking with their significant other. Of course, if one member
of the couple is using pornography far more than the other, there
is the possibility that he or she could become more detached from
the relationship. There is also the potential that if there is not an
open dialogue about pornography use, one person in the relationship could begin to feel insecure about their appearance or their
ability to satisfy their partner sexually.

The obvious difference between pornography of long ago and
the vivid and overwhelming number of videos at our fingertips nowadays might be the lack of imagination that comes from porn today.
With the vivid images of internet porn, there is a passive component to merely watching rather than using imagination and fantasy
to potentially be aroused. Some might argue that the whole exercise
of pornography is fantasy in and of itself and that certainly could
be true. Neurologically, there are a series of nerve pathways in our
brains that help us decipher our experiences. When a sexual experience is satisfying, our brains create a new pathway from that experience to what we are feeling. These brain pathways enable us to repeat
this experience because it feels so good. The potential problem with
pornography is that if we are constantly engaging with it, then our

brains make the connection to porn, sometimes at the expense of real sexual experiences with another human being. This could lead to lower arousal or loss of interest in having sex with others. These issues are found to be common for people of all ages who are regularly consuming pornography.

Is Porn Good or Bad?

Many argue that the constant exposure to pornography, including the sexual fantasies and perhaps better-than-average-looking people, can create unrealistic expectations in people who regularly consume it. If you are constantly watching beautiful people have amazing sex, then what happens when you cannot find (or attract) any of those beautiful people in real life? Or, if you attract one of them, what if the sex is not as good as it appears online? With the onslaught of videos available to just about anyone, combined with our short attention spans, particularly when online, we can find ourselves moving from one video to another for any host of reasons. It is much tougher to do that in real life with a long-term partner or spouse. You cannot just find another sexual partner immediately to satisfy you.

Pornography is readily available for us at any given time via the internet. Decades ago, people had to rent DVDs or video cassettes at video stores, and before that they had to visit movie theatres. People can now view porn anonymously and safely at home, which creates some of both the positives and the negatives discussed here. Like other topics throughout the book, there is an added element of friction when it comes to the availability of porn and our habits to consume it. It is very easy to find a site for pornography rather than go to a video store, which was common just a few decades ago. This lack of friction could lead individuals to regularly satisfy their impulses. Just like with anything else, "too much" is in the eye of the beholder, but regular access to pornography likely has an impact on consumption. If it is easier to access, one can assume that at least some will access it more frequently. For decades, there was also the belief that pornography incites men towards sexual violence, but the data from both eastern Europe in the 1960s as well as in the U.S. today does not support that argument. Since pornography became more readily available to consumers via the internet, sexual violence has dropped 44%. As Michael Castleman, a journalist who has written about sexuality for over four decades, writes, "Why would social ills decline as porn becomes more widely available? No one knows. But the one thing porn *really* causes is masturbation. Internet porn keeps men at home one-handing it. As a result, they're not out in the world acting irresponsibly or criminally." One could argue that there are other factors that may impact some of these numbers and that is likely the case. However, the availability of porn has not increased those numbers, as many might have suspected.

The most common question concerning pornography is whether it is beneficial or harmful to individuals and couples. As Ludden states, "Porn is neither good nor bad in itself. Rather, the issue is in how people use it. I think a good analogy here is alcohol. Many people consume alcohol responsibly, and they find that doing so greatly enhances their quality of life and their enjoyment of social interactions. However, some people abuse alcohol, [and] in the process, create great problems in their lives, wrecking their careers and destroying their families. Alcohol is neither good nor bad, but people can use it to achieve good or bad ends. I think we need to view pornography in the same way." There are a number of factors that impact whether pornography is good or bad, including the nature of couples' relationships or even the amount of consumption for a single person and whether that consumption might negatively impact other aspects of one's life. As with alcohol, being aware of the potential pitfalls of both consumption and overconsumption can be useful. For others, it might be something that is completely forbidden. Like so much else, each of us has to decide what works best for us.

CHAPTER 19

Publisher or Platform?

I n the fall of 1994, an unidentified user on a bulletin board titled *Money Talk* accused the New York–based investment firm Stratton Oakmont (depicted in the 2013 Leonardo DiCaprio movie *The Wolf of Wall Street*) and its CEO of criminal and fraudulent conduct associated with an initial public offering. *Money Talk* was a bulletin board developed and maintained by the internet service provider Prodigy. The investment firm sued Prodigy (and the unidentified user) for defamation. Prodigy argued that it could not be held responsible for content that was posted by its users. The plaintiff argued differently, suggesting that Prodigy was the actual publisher of this content and should therefore be held liable for it. The court found Prodigy liable for this content because, among other reasons, it was exercising editorial control in a number of different ways, including the removal of offensive language by users on its site. This ruling was a huge deal for the young internet, as it could potentially open the doors for hundreds if not thousands of lawsuits and likely threaten the existence of the World Wide Web as we once knew it. At the same time, CompuServe was sued by a third party for defamation. Their approach was not to moderate any content. Given this model of hands-off moderation, the lawsuit against them was thrown out.

These examples highlight two very different approaches to the internet with different rulings. However, these lawsuits signaled a new issue with regard to how content on the internet was characterized and if, and when, it was to be moderated. The First Amendment of the U.S. Constitution limits the government's ability to restrict forms of speech. So any law that would require tech companies to moderate content based upon a number of topics would most likely be viewed as unconstitutional and not make it into law. However, with open platforms where users can post any content they wish, there is a desire on the part of tech companies to eliminate content that might be hateful or pornographic.

Section 230

Washington, in response, created Section 230 of the Communications Act. The bill, which passed in 1996, states, "No provider or user of an interactive computer service shall be treated as the publisher or speaker of any information provided by another information content provider." Essentially, that means that online functionalities that host or promote any type of content are protected against any laws that would otherwise hold them legally responsible. It also allowed online platforms to remove content that they felt to be "otherwise objectionable," meaning content that is obscene, violent, or illustrates or promotes some sort of harassment. There are, of course, exceptions to Section 230 related to sex trafficking, intellectual property, and wiretapping statutes. In general, Section 230 allows users to post videos onto YouTube, review restaurants on Yelp, and post and repost all types of content onto Facebook without any legal issues for the website or app. The First Amendment of the U.S. Constitution is limited to free speech. Without Section 230, the first amendment would not protect tech companies that still wanted to moderate obscene content. Section 230 of this act has been interpreted that operators of internet services are not to be considered publishers, and therefore not responsible for the content provided on their sites by users.

The very existence of much of the web is based upon user content. The purpose of so many platforms, including social media, are designed so that users can post videos of their cute little puppies as well as their thoughts regarding any number of topics without any type of drawn-out curation process. If friends want to comment during the Academy Awards, it would not be worthwhile to post something during the ceremony and then have it sent to a moderator who would check it and approve it three days later. As Eric Goldman, professor at the Santa Clara University School of Law and co-director of the High Tech Law Institute, says, "Section 230 says that Facebook, YouTube, and other social media services have the same legal protection whether they function as a publisher of third-party content or as a platform for that content. This legal principle is why we as consumers are able to enjoy social media at all. Without Section 230, at minimum, social media services would need to pre-review all user submissions for legal risk – a process that would eliminate the immediacy of conversations on social media. More likely, social media services would only provide publication tools to a small subset of content producers; or most likely, they would simply cease to exist." Using humans to moderate content is both time consuming and expensive and does not permit the free flow of information and posts that exist within social media and a host of other sites across the web. Twitter alone receives close to half a billion posts per day. It seems impossible to imagine a scenario where all of that information would be monitored for accuracy. The same would hold true for YouTube, Facebook, or any other platform where users provide content. Added to that, who would make the editorial decisions regarding what information is true and what is false?

Tech companies promote themselves as instruments of free expression, a meeting place for people to communicate and share ideas on their platforms. Unlike broadcasters or publishers who have a responsibility for the content they produce, tech companies have argued that they are just the platform itself and nothing more. Tech companies are supportive of Section 230 because without it, they would be vulnerable to lawsuits from any user who feels as if they were wronged in some way by information posted by a user. In 2019, a video of U.S. House Speaker Nancy Pelosi giving a speech at an event was altered, making it appear as if she were speaking more slowly and giving the impression that she was intoxicated. To many, it was obvious that the video had been distorted and shared on tech platforms such as Facebook. According to the *Washington Post*, the video was posted by a conservative Facebook page called WatchDog, where it had been viewed more than two million times within one day and shared more than 45,000 times, with numerous comments calling her "drunk" and "a babbling mess." Responding to a backlash as to why this distorted content would be continuously distributed on Facebook, Head of Policy at Facebook Monika Bickert said, "We don't have a policy that stipulates that the information you post on Facebook must be true."

Section 230 essentially supports that position, allowing big tech companies not to be held liable for content that might be false, even while the big tech company is overseeing content that could potentially be harmful in some way. As tech companies have increased in size, so has their impact on many aspects of our lives. More Americans are receiving their news and information from social media. With information coming from users, who may or may not be identifiable, there are more possibilities for misinformation, whether through bias, bad sources, or purposeful propaganda of sorts. The implications of large segments of the population receiving misinformation are significant, whether related to politics, health vaccinations, or any host of other topics. This raises a number of questions regarding the responsibility of platforms potentially to monitor the content that users post. Does YouTube have a responsibility to take down content that supports wild conspiracy theories, whether in support of the right or the left? Should Facebook host information that they know is patently false and potentially, as we have seen in previous years, impactful to our democratic process?

User content on these platforms heightens the possibilities of the creation of echo chambers and confirmation bias from users. If a certain group has a political agenda to misinform the public regarding a certain topic, they can (and do) repeatedly use YouTube, Facebook, and Twitter to spread their message. If a user sides politically with this group that is spreading this disinformation, it can reinforce their beliefs, creating a snowball effect. The implications of this misinformation can be serious. Researchers from four universities surveyed 21,000 individuals during the COVID-19 pandemic to explore attitudes and behaviors related to the virus as well as where the users received their information. Respondents were asked whether they believed 11 false claims, whether related to preventative treatments, conspiracy theories, or risk factors that had been circulated across the web during the pandemic; 28% of Snapchat users, 25% of Wikipedia users, and 23% of Instagram users believed at least some of the inaccurate claims. There were similar numbers for users who received information from Facebook messenger (26%) and WhatsApp (31%). In contrast, the respondents who received their information from local television, news websites, or newspapers had the lowest levels of misinformation (11%) about the virus. The implications of this misinformation can contribute to less likelihood of wearing a mask, seeking treatment for COVID, or perhaps even voluntarily receiving a potential vaccine to immunize from the virus. As we all know, misinformation has real consequences that can cost lives.

To me, the notion of whether a site is a publisher or a platform is the equivalent of two different types of dinner parties. First, if you host a dinner party and cook all the dishes, you plan for each course carefully. You may decide how the entrée will work with the appetizers and select a wine based upon whether you're serving chicken or steak. To plan the perfect meal, you would think about the food allergens of your guests as well as any dietary restrictions. This is what a publisher essentially does. They create the content and have a responsibility for all of it since they are involved in the development and any review process that oversees it. The second dinner party is the potluck. I do not cook much, so this is the route I usually select. Here, you invite friends to come to dinner and tell them to bring their favorite dish, or if you're like me, to bring any dish. With this route, you are not involved in the planning of how the entrées and appetizers might work together and you are certainly not thinking about the dietary restrictions of your guests. Sally could be allergic to peanuts and James may bring a bag of peanuts as his dish! In this scenario, you are a platform (almost literally as you might be merely providing the table for the dinner). If something goes wrong and all the guests bring desserts, you may or may not be held responsible. If Sally sees the bag of peanuts at the table, she will certainly avoid them and not think how terrible a host you are, but rather how thoughtless someone (we probably all know it is James) was in bringing a contribution that they bought at the 7-11.

In an open letter to Facebook CEO Mark Zuckerberg, U.S. Senator Michael Bennet said, "Globally, misuse of Facebook platforms appears to be growing worse." Last year, the Oxford Internet Institute reported that governments or political parties orchestrated "social media manipulation" campaigns in 70 countries in 2019 (up from 28 in 2017 and 48 in 2018). Oxford found that at least 26 authoritarian regimes used social media "as a tool of information control . . . [and] to suppress fundamental human rights, discredit political opponents, and drown out dissenting opinions." It reported that Facebook was authoritarians' "platform of choice."

Bennet called upon Facebook to develop a plan to limit hate speech, add more content reviewers, and take steps to address political misinformation. It seems as if it is only a matter of time before the government decides to make significant changes to Section 230. As Goldman states, "Section 230 is on the endangered watch list. Government regulators have decided that they must 'fix' the internet, and their efforts to fix the internet will certainly include revisions to Section 230. Unfortunately, most government regulators view the internet only as a threat, and they are prepared to sacrifice everything we love about the internet in a quest – most likely futile – to eliminate the perceived threats. There is a massive disconnect, then, between most consumers who love the internet and value it highly in their lives and government regulators who are working hard – and against their constituents' interests – to take all of that away."

Several bills have been proposed that would either alter or eliminate Section 230. The content of those bills ranges from the requirement of more transparency for big tech companies in how they edit and remove content to more oversight of content for larger tech companies that meet a certain threshold of users or even annual revenue. President Trump signed an Executive Order preventing online censorship that called upon the Federal Communications Commission (FCC) to reinterpret Section 230 as well as the Federal Trade Commission (FTC) to monitor and potentially prohibit any unfair moderation practices. It would also allow users to take legal action if the terms of service have somehow been violated. There are significant issues with this Executive Order, most notably the ability of the order even to ask the FCC and FTC to take any action whatsoever. Upon entering office, President Biden has also stated that changes need to be made to Section 230. The January 6 insurrection at the U.S. Capitol was a direct representation of some of the misinformation that circulates on these platforms. Many of the conspiracy theories associated with the 2020 presidential election continued to grow on platforms, raising anger among individuals who were being fed these unfounded claims. In response, many social media platforms banned President Donald Trump permanently. Those on the right side of the aisle view this as a direct assault on free speech, while those on the left see it as a first step in addressing some of the misinformation that tends to live within these platforms. With this shared unhappiness, albeit for different reasons, it is difficult to envision a future where Section 230 does not look significantly different in the near future.

The Future of the Internet

So where do we go from here? What will happen when it comes to new laws that might help address some of these issues? As Goldman says, "When Congress is done 'fixing' Section 230, we will see the end of the user-generated content era of the internet (what has often been called Web 2.0). In its place, we will see the emergence of Web 3.0, which will be principally professionally produced content made available behind paywalls (where the paywall fees will be used in part to compensate the professional content producers). In other words, Web 3.0 will look a lot like how the cable industry looked in the 1990s, or how Netflix looks today. I love Netflix, but it's not the internet – but Netflix-style services will be all we have left to enjoy on the internet and only after we pay a greater amount of our income to gain access." This approach will certainly limit the democratization of the web, which for the last few decades has provided everyone a platform to share their voice. However, as we discussed in previous chapters, users are now paying for content through their attention, whether via push notifications or a host of ads and other marketing tactics. With this new potential Web 3.0, it is unclear whether users would pay with both their wallets and their attention. It seems difficult to imagine a future where platforms would not want a share of both.

There are a host of actions that citizens can take to influence the future of the web. As Goldman states, "Find out if your elected officials are working on internet policy or supporting other politicians' work. If so, find out if they are supporting regulations that would damage the internet and ask them for empirical evidence demonstrating that their efforts will solve the purported problems and not cause unwanted collateral damage. Simply letting your politicians know that you care about the internet and want them to fight for an open internet will go a long way. Simply put, they never hear that message from their constituents, and they assume their constituents want them to burn down the current internet. Tell them they are wrong."

When it comes to Web 3.0, we do not have to "throw the baby out with the bathwater." We can thoughtfully make changes that address elements of misinformation yet still offer many of the same benefits that the web provides us. Like with anything, if we want our politicians to be thoughtful, we have to provide them with our thoughts! As we rely more and more upon platforms that generate content from users, we will need to be more proactive in this discourse regarding Section 230, as well as continue to look critically at content that is posted across the web. As discussed in an earlier chapter, we should always examine the sources of our news, ensuring that they are reliable and transparent with their reporting. We should question conspiracy theories and even be vigilant when it comes to our position within any form of echo chambers in which we may participate. Conversely, we can push both government and tech companies to develop transparent policies regarding what stays and what gets removed on the platforms. Section 230 was the fertilizer that brought the web as we know it to fruition. It has real problems that need to be addressed, but we can potentially do so in a thoughtful manner that limits both disinformation and censorship while still giving us the cute little puppy videos that we all love.

CHAPTER 20

Algorithms

My Grandma Eunice makes the best blueberry pie. I don't know how she does it, but if you eat it warm with vanilla ice cream, you have yourself a winner. Not long ago it occurred to me that Grandma uses an algorithm to make that pie. It was not that she somehow used TikTok to make the pie or had some kitchen robot assist her. (She is not one for technology. The iPad we bought her for Christmas a few years back has made a lovely, expensive coaster for her coffee). Nevertheless, an algorithm is essentially "a set of guidelines to describe how to perform a task." It can be a recipe for blueberry pie, or code programmed into social media or a department store website.

The term "algorithm" is thrown about a great deal. It is always seen as a creature that lives within large computers and knows many things about us. This is actually kind of true, except the creature part. We see algorithms in all parts of our lives, but usually as codes that tell computers what to do, and they usually consist of words like "and," "then," and "or." Algorithms are used within social media, entertainment, police stations, hospitals, and just about anywhere else decisions of some sort are being made. Algorithms use our past behavior to tell us what to look at on social media and what to watch on Netflix. Based upon what we viewed previously, there is a good chance that we will like this or that. Algorithms are put into place so that we will stay on the website or social media platform for as long as possible, or will purchase the recommended products on Amazon or Target. They also tell doctors how to diagnose patients, using an extensive database of past patients with similar medical data. Algorithms automate so much of our lives, from stock trading to the booking of travel. They assist advertisers in serving us ads on all of our devices that are based upon the sites we have visited and the type of social media posts with which we engage. We have all experienced the phenomenon where we perform a Google search for running shoes and suddenly there are ads for running shoes as banners on websites and within our social media feeds.

Algorithms in Our Daily Lives

There are definite benefits to the use of algorithms. First, they can make decisions far more rapidly than humans, analyzing large amounts of data in a fraction of the time that it would take a human to perform the same task. Second, there is an element of objectivity when it comes to algorithms that you do not necessarily get with humans. Although it does not eliminate all bias, algorithms can be far less biased than humans. Algorithms provide a great advantage in suggesting content and ads that are most relevant to us, saving us time and making our social media journey more enjoyable. Algorithms, and hence tech, know us far better than do most of the people in our lives. Pandora knows the songs we like, Amazon knows when it is time to buy more diapers for the baby, and as we discussed, Facebook and YouTube know the content we like to keep up with on their sites as much as possible. As Andrew Tutt, a Washington, D.C.,–based attorney and author of the paper "An FDA for Algorithms," explains, "There are a whole lot of things that would simply be impossible without algorithms. Modern search engines and social networks simply would not work at all without algorithms. And these technologies have been some of the most transformative in human history – making information available to more people than ever before and bringing people together in ways they never could before. These kinds of emergent technologies – technologies that do entirely new things – are the number one benefit of algorithms."

Predictive policing is the idea that police can essentially forecast a crime and be present to stop it before the crime even takes place.

One can use a variety of analyses based upon previous crimes to determine where crime will occur in the future. They can pinpoint certain neighborhoods, or perhaps even vacant buildings within those neighborhoods, that are more likely to experience crime for one reason or another. Of course, it is important to note that predictive policing (or any algorithm for that matter) is only as good as the data feeding the algorithm, as well as the objectivity of the human interpreting it. Prediction is not always accurate. And perhaps in some cases, even if the data are accurate and the human is unbiased in their analysis of the data, there are still challenges. H.V. Jagadish, director of the Michigan Institute for Data Science, wrote in *Slate* magazine, "Suppose you fit the profile of a bad driver and have accumulated points on your driving record. Consider how you would feel if you had a patrol car follow you every time you got behind the wheel. Even worse, it's likely, even if you're doing your best, that you will make an occasional mistake. For most of us, rolling through a stop sign or driving five miles per hour above the speed limit is usually of little consequence. But since you have a cop following you, you get a ticket for every small offense. In consequence, you end up with an even worse driving record." He reminds readers that a probabilistic prediction is not certain and there are real implications – in many cases, civil liberties concerns – when innocent people are charged with crimes based upon probabilities.

Many people have concerns about potential bias when it comes to the use of algorithms. In 2018, Pew found that 58% of Americans felt that the use of algorithms will reflect the biases of those who created them. There are three main sources of bias that occur from algorithms. First, the initial data that feeds the system is either problematic or could represent some sort of bias. If, for example, an institution is looking to select students based upon a statistical analysis of current and past successful students to determine who will be accepted in the future, there could be a number of problems. Are the metrics that defined success for the current and past students accurate? Could there have been a bias on the part of the faculty who were providing grades? Also, what if there were major weaknesses in the curriculum? If the curriculum is not adequate for some reason, why would you base the success of future students on it? In addition, the metrics that the algorithm is using may not be the correct ones. The second form of bias is technical, where the limitations of the design of a program demonstrate some element of bias, whether purposefully or not. For example, a website might share only the top or first five recommendations for new shoes or vacation packages when there are actually hundreds, creating an illusion that the five listed are the only ones. Finally, emergent biases can occur when algorithms are used in areas for which they may not have originally been designed or when the algorithm has not been designed to take important new knowledge into consideration.

Over one billion hours of YouTube videos are watched each day. Of those total videos, 70% of that watch time is from recommended videos. So if you're good at math, that means 700,000,000 hours of videos are viewed based upon the recommendations coming from YouTube algorithms. That is a lot of hours, and as we have discussed throughout this book, the longer people stay on their site or app, the more revenue is collected. Therefore, the algorithm or AI recommendations are very important. The more videos you watch on YouTube, the more of a profile the algorithm builds of you, working to determine future videos that it thinks you will like based upon past viewing. It will consider the channels and topics you have watched in the past; how much time you spend viewing; and how many times the videos have been recommended to a particular person. What is important to remember here is that the videos are not recommended based upon quality or even accuracy, but whether or not they will be watched. YouTube has the objective of finding you the right video based upon your search and keeping you on the site for as long as possible.

Since the algorithms within YouTube are designed to recommend videos that you have a preference for, there are a number of potential harmful outcomes. First, if you are only watching videos that you agree with politically, you will be recommended other videos that have a similar bias. For example, if you search a video where a Republican or a Democrat is getting "owned," you will likely get more videos showcasing such scenarios. Based upon whichever party you have a preference for, the algorithm might start recommending videos on topics such as gun control, abortion, or immigration. The algorithm will continue to build a profile of you as you watch more videos to continue to feed you content that supports a certain bias. Conspiracy theories – a related issue – can be very popular on YouTube. In many cases, the people who support such theories do not watch mainstream news but rather just social media and YouTube. All of the information they are getting is, first, shared with them to keep them on the site and, second, not necessarily vetted or examined for accuracy. As more conspiracy theory videos are recommended and then watched, they get even more recommendations since they are more popular. This creates a vicious cycle that may or may not have anything to do with the truth. In some cases, users can find themselves going down a rabbit hole, where one recommended video leads a user to watch more and more videos from the same video creator. They can potentially then subscribe to the channel and ultimately buy into whatever conspiracy theory is being promoted. Echo chambers ensue.

As Tutt explains, "Algorithms are partly responsible for reinforcing biases and creating echo chambers throughout society. But ultimate responsibility rests with their designers. Today's algorithms reinforce biases because they have been built to do things like "optimize engagement" as a way of maximizing attention (which translates to profit). The analogy is junk food. The makers of junk food do not want to give people heart disease; they just want to maximize the number of people who buy their food. Algorithms that reinforce biases are the junk food of the internet." As Tristan Harris explained to *Wired* magazine, "You open up that YouTube video your friend sends you after your lunch break. You come back to your computer and you think, *OK, I know those other times I ended up watching two or three videos and getting sucked into it, but this time it's going to be really different. I'm just going to watch this one video . . .* , and then somehow, that's not what happens. You wake up from a trance three hours later and say, 'What the hell just happened?' And it's because you didn't realize you had a supercomputer pointed at your brain. So when you open up that video, you're activating Google's billions of dollars of computing power and they've looked at what has ever gotten two billion human animals to click on another video. And it knows way more about what's going to be the perfect chess move to play against your mind. If you think of your mind as a chessboard, and you think you know the perfect move to play – *I'll just watch this one video*. But you can only see so many moves ahead on the chessboard. But the computer sees your mind and it says, 'No, no, no. I've played a billion simulations of this chess game before on these other human animals watching YouTube,' and it's going to win." The chess analogy that Harris uses is apt. As discussed in earlier chapters, it is indeed a competition because we have different goals than the technology. Our goal is to watch that one video on YouTube and then move on with our day. The objective of YouTube, or any other algorithm, is to keep us on the screen as much as possible, suggesting videos that we are inclined to watch. Each time we watch or like something, the social network has more information to help it serve us more content and of course, more ads. Facebook can track where we browse within other sites that have plugins with Facebook. In addition, if you use your Facebook sign-on to enter another site to log in, all of that information goes to Facebook as well. As Harris states, "That's the most duplicitous part. If you want to know what Facebook is, imagine a priest in a confession booth, and they listened to two billion people's confessions. But they also watch you around your whole day, what you click on, which ads of Coca-Cola or Pepsi, or the shirtless man and the shirtless women, and all your conversations that you have with everybody else in your life – because they have Facebook Messenger, they have that data too – but imagine that this priest in a confession booth, their entire business model, is to sell access to the confession booth to another party. So someone else can manipulate you. Because that's the only way that this priest makes money in this case. So they don't make money any other way."

There is a distinction between algorithms and machine learning. Algorithms are basically developed by a set of rules: "if this, then that." Machine learning, on the other hand, is developed through an audit and/or statistical analyses of large data sets. For example, a university could use machine learning to try to predict success of applicants into their schools. Through machine learning, they could do an analysis of the attributes of the top performing students currently enrolled and, through that information, develop a way to sort new applicants who may possess those same attributes. However, the performance of the machine learning is only as good as the inputs. For example, if machine learning is used to determine which applicants to a college or university might be best suited for admission, there could be an objective process to determine a variety of variables that would select students based upon a given criteria. However, if some of the variables that were inputs into the machine learning system were biased or subjective in nature, then the performance of the machine learning would be compromised. In this example, applicants from inner-city or rural schools might be at a disadvantage because the system only recognizes certain achievement metrics that are only found in wealthier private or suburban schools. Like with research data, the old saying of "garbage in, garbage out" applies. The process is only as good as what is going into it.

Whenever your online decisions and preferences are being used to recommend other content, privacy is an issue. For example, if we search for a particular drug, we are now identified as potentially being sick. In her book *Hello World, Being Human in the Age of Algorithms,* Hannah Fry says, "Every time you shop online, every time you sign-up for a newsletter, or register on a website, or inquire about a new car, or fill out a warranty card, or buy a new home, or register to vote – every time you hand over any data at all – your information is being collected and sold to a data broker. Remember when you told an estate agent what kind of property you were looking for? Sold to a data broker. Or those details you once typed into an insurance comparison website? Sold to a data broker. In some cases, even your entire browser history can be bundled and sold to a data broker." Companies can buy these data and based upon it, infer certain behaviors about you, from the type of driver you are, to your sexual orientation, to a host of other personal variables, all of which could impact everything from insurance rates to loan applications. Fry reminds us that anytime there is a free site of some sort, we have to think twice about what we are providing. There is indeed no free lunch!

As part of a Pew Research study, several scholars and leaders from both the public and private sector outlined a series of steps that can be taken to ensure that algorithms are fair, transparent, and can minimize any potential harmful societal consequences. These principles include someone who is externally identified who is responsible for any adverse consequences of the algorithm, a non-technical explanation of the process that the algorithm takes in making decisions, as well as identification of any accuracy issues, and the ability to evaluate the efficacy of the algorithm through regular or non-regular audits. Developers of algorithms should not create any discriminatory or unjust impacts, specifically when looking at their efficacy relative to specific demographics such as race, sex, and so on. Finally, the public should have a better understanding of algorithms both from the perspective of process and implications. As part of that study, David Lankes, a professor and director at the University of South Carolina School of Library and Information Science, wrote, "There is simply no doubt that an aggregate, automation and large-scale application of algorithms have had a net-positive effect. People can be more productive, know more about more topics than ever before, identify trends in massive piles of data and better understand the world around them. That said, unless there is an increased effort to make true information literacy a part of basic education, there will be a class of people who can use algorithms and a class used by algorithms."

Algorithm Oversight?

There has been much discussion about the need for regulation of algorithms. As Tutt states, "Algorithmic regulation and transparency is definitely needed. In the realm of search engines and social media, it may not be that *government* regulation (defined as regulation by the states or federal government) is the right approach. But regulation rooted in *democratic accountability* is needed even if it does not come from the government. Democratic accountability in that currently search engines and social media platforms are optimized to serve a narrow set of commercial values (e.g. to maximize profit). That leads corporations to create algorithms that have harmful side effects because they cause high levels of engagement. To protect against those harmful side effects to our society, those platforms should take into account *more values* than merely maximizing profits – and in fact should take into account the ways in which the biases and echo chambers they create produce harmful byproducts." Social media sites and search engines can also utilize external advisory boards that could both provide some oversight to algorithms as well as address any issues associated with user privacy. Tutt suggests that these groups do not need to be set by the government but rather seated and run by the users themselves. As he explains, "The analogy would be to laws mandating that workers own a certain percentage of companies in some countries – it ensures a form of accountability that the structures of modern platforms currently lack."

Algorithms do lots of things for us in our daily lives, from telling us what to read to whom to interact with on social media, and they even help us with medical diagnoses and fighting crime. However, we should not blindly follow their instructions, but rather critically look at what they are suggesting. Following regular recommendations can lead us into echo chambers where we are only looking at content based upon past consumption. Each algorithm is only as good as those who are building it. If the people building the algorithm are biased, there is a greater chance that the algorithm will be biased. We should also be mindful when it comes to when and where we share our personal data, knowing that it could be shared to lots of places to use it for a variety of reasons. It seems that for medicine, financial services, and a host of other professions, the analysis of big data to help make decisions and eliminate some of the transactional components of the professions is useful. However, the empathy, listening, and understanding that come from a physician who has used an algorithm to make a difficult diagnosis is very much needed when she has to deliver that diagnosis to the patient. In many cases, the human element is critical, whether in partnership with the professional or in overseeing the inputs and analyses of the algorithm to ensure objectivity and fairness. If we think critically and examine both the inputs and outputs to ensure fairness and transparency, algorithms indeed can serve us in many positive ways, whether it is fighting crime, curing disease, finding a potential mate, or simply the recipe for Grandma's blueberry pie.

CHAPTER 21

Regaining the Feeling

The information that I shared in this book brings with it significant complications. On the one hand, we live in an information age where we have access to enough knowledge to fuel new experiences and creative endeavors that, until recently, were beyond our imagination. This democratization of information provides immense opportunities for most to learn, work, and connect in very tangible ways. We have the information, and the technical platforms that go along with it, to actively invest our money, plan intricate details of our vacations, and even watch video footage of the raccoon outside our front door that loves our leftovers. Through this information, we have the capacity both to know and to learn, heightening our awareness regarding events near and far and fueling our knowledge regarding matters that have direct impact on our families and friends. Not only do we have the power to choose what we want to know but also when we want to know it. We can take courses when we want to learn, stream videos at the exact moment we want to be entertained, and know the precise temperature of just about anywhere on the globe at the exact moment we want to know it. The old saying is that knowledge is power, so these technical gadgets that produce this information are a strong dose of steroids. Added to that, we are not only consumers of information but creators of it as well. Through various platforms on the web, we can share our perspective regarding the serious and the trivial for the world to view, whether it is selfies, links to conspiracy theories and personality assessments, or calls for community action. YouTube gives us a front-row seat to "how the sausage is made" when it comes to our democratic process, the creation of important vaccines, or how sausage is actually made! We post a review about everything from our best dinner experience to our worst pet groomer experience and everything in between. If someone wants to share it, they can share it, and we can view it.

As we all know, more information does not necessarily equate to better information. With these open platforms, anyone with an opinion has the ability to share that opinion – informed, biased, or otherwise. The media landscape also provides multiple audience segments to find the story or opinion that reaffirms their position, making for, at best, suspect information. Open platforms make it inexpensive to share information but expensive to share trustworthy information, that is, information that has been vetted through some sort of editorial process. Opinion and sensationalism sell and there is less of a motivation to edit and recheck facts than there is to be first to report, making for sensationalism and bias at the expense of facts and quality data. With all of this information and the ability to create and share, it seems virtually impossible to determine the relevant from the irrelevant, fact from fiction, bias from objective. The sensationalized nature of news is designed to draw our attention to the next story. Graphic videos of human tragedy keep us glued to the screens. The term "breaking news" elicits a shot of dopamine, so it is announced with trumpets blaring and flashy graphics all the time, even if it is not breaking news. Clickbait headlines draw us into stories with headlines that distort actual content, altering perceptions of actual events. So many people now receive their news from social media, making the truth sometimes even more difficult to discern from reality. The sensationalized nature of news today creates compassion fatigue among viewers, where we become numb to the suffering of others, impacting our capacity to respond whether in-person or by donating to charities far away.

No longer are the boundaries to our success, productivity, and wonder dictated by the amount of information that we have available to us. Rather, we are now constrained by the limits of our attention, that scarce and important resource that fuels our consciousness.

When we focus our attention on any one given item, it is at the expense of other items. As Herbert Simon stated, "We have to be efficient in where we allocate our attention within this information-rich world." We all think we can multitask effectively, but the reality is that we struggle to divide our limited attention among two tasks. Whether on social media or watching network television, we are paying for these platforms with our attention. For anyone or anything to grab your attention among the sea of information, there has to be something attractive that makes it stand out among other forms of information. For technology developers, there is an objective to keep users on their platforms for as long as possible. These platforms are designed to deliver users to advertisers, increasing the revenue of these platforms.

There are a number of steps that we can take to mitigate the pitfalls of this information age. Through the contributions of professionals researching and treating individuals facing many of these challenges, I have outlined a number of actions that each of us can consider in managing the information that permeates countless aspects of our lives. Some of these steps require both a change in habit as well as thoughtful reflection.

Reflecting

We can proactively alter our environment to manage our own attention. The presence of our smartphone has a significant impact on our capacity to focus and is a source of distraction for many of us. It does not have to be in front of us all of the time, draining our cognitive capacity and making us overly available to every push notification that comes our way. In the office, we can eliminate the constant vigilance that tends to be associated with our email inboxes by closing Outlook folders during times where we want to focus and by prioritizing emails and other forms of communication to curb information overload. Many organizations have now developed "email hours" to limit the amount of time that employees are engaged with their inbox, helping them focus their attention on creativity and even more in-person communication. We do not always have to make ourselves available, whether through email, social media, or our smartphone. Having time to reflect, whether alone or with our partner, can be incredibly beneficial to both our work and our relationships. We can limit push notifications, delete unnecessary apps that are vying for our attention, and even choose to call friends or colleagues rather than text. Although a phone call can require more of our attention, the benefits of hearing others' voices can be more beneficial and potentially limit the further back and forth of future emails and texts, which much of the time are superficial and less than authentic.

We can protect ourselves from the sensationalized and sometimes highly opinionated nature of news. Not only can we manage our consumption of all of it, but we can pick one cause and put our energy and resources behind it rather than ruminating about the state of current events. Whether it is volunteering at an animal shelter in response to headlines related to animal abuse or coordinating a recycling campaign in response to climate change, we can take our anxiety and turn it into something positive. The opinionated nature of some news today can lead us down roads of confirmation bias, echo chambers, and tribalism. Feeling empathy towards other human beings, even if they are not necessarily part of our "tribe," can go a long way in breaking through those filter bubbles. Remembering that the people we interact with online all have a family, hopes, and dreams like the rest of us can help us see people, and potentially current events, through a more objective lens.

This book has focused extensively on reward systems that are part of much of the information that we come into contact with daily. We receive a shot of dopamine when we get an email or text, or even hear of breaking news. The reward structure that is established within social media provides for a variable rewards schedule, meaning that we are unsure when the reward, usually a like or comment from another user, will occur. We post a selfie on Instagram and want to see how many people will like it. We post pictures of our vacation and want other users to be impressed that we are going to some exotic place or experiencing something that is different and perhaps better than others. We see the same phenomenon with echo chambers, where like-minded individuals come together relative to a specific topic, whether politics, sports, or others, on social media. In order to get the same level of affirmation, users post what can become increasingly polarized viewpoints to gain the attention and affirmation of other users. With all of these scenarios, we log on, post, comment, and return, seeing if what we said, how we looked, or what we did was somehow accepted by others. Examining the authenticity that comes from this affirmation on social media can help us determine whether it is the best use of our time and attention. The people with whom we connect on these platforms make a huge difference as well, because they can be effective in bringing us closer to those we know but potentially detrimental if we are connecting with strangers, leading us to feelings of FOMO and unrealistic comparisons between our lives and the potentially curated lives of strangers.

As we consider the overwhelming number of choices that we face in many aspects of our lives, we can first place parameters around the amount of time that we are willing to dedicate to making those choices. In deciding upon a vacation destination, we can force ourselves to make a decision within a week or a month, so that we collect information, talk to others, and come to a consensus within that time period. Obviously, the exception is if the journey to make the selection is fun. If we enjoy looking at potential new homes, then being a maximizer – one who desires to explore all possibilities through visiting open houses and online listings – is a good thing. However, being a maximizer regarding every possible choice in our lives can be nothing short of overwhelming. How would we even make it out of the first aisle of the grocery store? Second, we can filter our choices, and the sea of information that goes along with them, through online comments about products, experiences, and restaurants. Finally, knowing that our decisions are not necessarily all-or-nothing can help ease the pressure of making that decision. If you and your partner waffle endlessly about which movie to go see, it is easier to remind each other that if you do not like it, you can leave. The same holds true for a career or relationship decision; we make the best decision we can with the data that we have available, and we move forward with it. If we need to readjust because it is not working for us, then we readjust. Learning from past decisions can help us in the future. Realizing that even the most important life decisions can be altered in some way, shape, or form if they do not work can help us from becoming immobilized in deciding upon a flavor of jam or a new car.

Reflection is key. I am not talking about a three-month journey to a mountain somewhere. Rather, I mean a short respite to consider how all of this information, and the technology that goes along with it, is really serving our goals and needs. We can weigh the benefits of whether curating aspects of our lives for connections, for friends, family, or strangers, is really worth the investment of time and attention. Do you feel closer to others through those platforms? Do those who are providing those rewards in the form of likes and comments know you better through this effort? Reflecting upon the sources of information that we engage with can also help us determine if we are well-informed regarding the news of the day. If our desire is to be objective, informed citizens, then examining both our sources of information as well as those with whom we engage could be a worthwhile exercise. Are you finding your biases and perspectives confirmed or challenged? Who is within your circle? Are there individuals who come from different backgrounds with differing opinions or have you unfriended everyone who sits across the political aisle from you? I hope that through this book, you recognize the deeper value of your own attention and the power that it brings to our lives. Realizing the value of our attention can help us determine where we want to spend it and, of course, invest it. Many of us constantly research the best places to invest our money, reading books and talking with others regarding where we can get the best return, whether for our retirement, our children's education, or any number of life goals. I hope this book has served as a source for how to invest your attention and where you might get the most out of it. Nowhere did I argue that there was a "sure bet." However, I hope that you received some insight on how to evaluate your own investing and spending of this valuable and personal commodity.

Empowerment

As mentioned earlier, the genesis for *Numb* came out of my own reflection regarding compassion for others. I found myself with less capacity to care for the people closest to me because of overall exhaustion with the bad news that I was exposed to on a regular basis. The compassion fatigue that I was feeling was a result of seeing and hearing the suffering of others via all kinds of information sources, without ever really doing anything about it. The realization that I did not want to be numb – or perhaps more importantly, that I wanted to be that helper in some way, shape, or form – drew me to learning more and writing this book that I hope will empower some of you who feel the same way. Not only can we manage our news consumption but, perhaps more importantly, we get out of our bubbles and pick a cause and do something about it. We are not helpless. Whether through compassion in helping others or channeling our outrage to create change, we have the ability to pick a cause and impact our world beyond hitting a "like," sharing a link, or just getting pissed off. For me, what I was doing – or actually, what I wasn't doing – was not advancing the causes that I cared about the most. As many of the experts I interviewed throughout this book stated, the information we receive should have some end goal in mind to make us better informed, whether as voters, investors, or helpers. In your reflection, if you are finding that information is merely a fuel for compassion fatigue or outrage, then maybe you have a great opportunity to make some change, both for yourself as well as for who and what is most important to you.

Unlike in similar books, it doesn't seem pragmatic to suggest that we should go on some sort of dopamine fast and abandon technology. That seems like an oversimplified approach to what is a complex problem. One of the other recurring themes throughout this book is moderation. Through moderation, maybe we could be more awake, focusing our attention on the world around us, rather than the screens that are constantly in front of us. We might be compelled to do more, to act beyond a tweet or a picture, to volunteer, donate, or just sit outside and talk with (or maybe even meet) the neighbors. Our circle of friends could come from places we volunteer or worship, creating authentic connections through authentic experiences. Instead of staring at our phones in a coffee shop, we might hear the perspective of the person sitting next to us whose view is different than our own. Perhaps that conversation would be empathetic and respectful because that view is coming from another human, one with similar hopes and dreams. We might never agree with that person on certain topics, but at minimum, we heard the other side of the issue and they heard ours.

We seem to have a better chance at achieving some element of common ground through this uncomplicated and very human approach. We can be awake even in the midst of this information age. We can use all of the approaches described throughout this book in ways to achieve larger goals for ourselves, whether in our work or in our relationships. We can utilize technology as a tool that leads us to productivity and creativity, as opposed to a quagmire of emails, instant messages, and conflicting information that mires us in brain fog. A tool that brings us closer to those we value, rather than a secondary residence where we spend a large amount of our waking hours superficially engaged. A tool that helps us make informed choices, whether in picking a new mattress or a life partner, rather than a mirage that depicts a level of perfection that reality just cannot produce. Each of us has our own goals, whether personally or professionally. We have to decide how we see these tools and platforms within those goals. Rather than all of it managing us, we can be proactive in managing all of it to help us get to where we want to go.

Over the course of writing this book, I often wondered whether, when we look back at all the time and attention spent on these platforms, we would say it was time well spent. "That four hours per day I spent on Facebook years ago really made me happy." I am not so sure. However, authenticity in both our experiences as well as our true selves was certainly a topic that came up again and again throughout this book. Social media, dating apps, and other sources of information often replace authentic experiences as opposed to leading us to them, even when our motivation to participate in these platforms in the first place is authenticity. All of this technology can bring us closer to other people or create lasting experiences, but they are better serving as tools rather than destinations. Habits can be difficult to break but each of us has the ability to change our environment to make it work for us. Whether this book is influential in you adding hours of additional time to social media or causes you to "get off the grid" entirely, I hope that however you decide to proceed, whether in your relationships, work, and every other aspect of your life, you have been able to reflect upon what is working for you, and, perhaps most importantly, feel empowered to regain the feeling.

References

Introduction

Abramovich, G. (2019, September 8). If You Think Email Is Dead, Think Again. *Adobe Blog*. https://blog.adobe.com/en/publish/2019/09/08/if-you-think-email-is-dead--think-again.html#gs.mniunm

Henderson, G. (2020, August 24). How Much Time Does the Average Person Spend on Social Media? *Digital Marketing Blog*. https://www.digitalmarketing.org/blog/how-much-time-does-the-average-person-spend-on-social-media

Molla, R. (2020, January 6). Tech companies tried to help us spend less time on our phones. It didn't work. *Recode*. https://www.vox.com/recode/2020/1/6/21048116/tech-companies-time-well-spent-mobile-phone-usage-data

Reed, E.A. (1996). *The Necessity of Experience*. Yale University Press.

Chapter 1: The Information Age

Cook, B. (n.d.). ESPNU College Football Podcast. Audio. ESPN.

Domo. (n.d.). Data Never Sleeps 5.0. Fact sheet. https://www.domo.com/learn/data-never-sleeps-5

Simon, H.A. (1971). Designing Organizations for an Information-Rich World. In M. Greenberger (Ed.), *Computers, Communications, and the Public Interest* (pp. 37–52). Johns Hopkins Press.

Turkle, S. (2011). *Alone Together: Why We Expect More from Technology and Less from Each Other*. Basic Books.

Chapter 2: Can I Have Your Attention Please?

Eyal, N. (2019). *Indistractable: How to Control Your Attention and Choose Your Life.* Bloomsbury Publishing.

Goldhaber, MH. (1997). The Attention Economy and the Net. *First Monday.* https://firstmonday.org/article/view/519/440

Goldman, A.L. (1982, April 26). Student Scores Rise After Nearby Subway is Quieted. *New York Times.* https://www.nytimes.com/1982/04/26/nyregion/student-scores-rise-after-nearby-subway-is-quieted.html

James, W. (1950). *The Principles of Psychology.* Dover Publications. (Originally published by Henry Holt and Company, 1890.)

Mark, G., Iqbal, S.T., Czerwinski, M., Johns, P., & Samo, A. (2016). Email Duration, Batching and Self-interruption: Patterns of Email Use on Productivity and Stress. *CHI '16: Proceedings of the 2016 CHI Conference on Human Factors in Computing Systems,* 1717–1728. https://affect.media.mit.edu/pdfs/16.Mark-CHI_Email.pdf

Yirka, B. (2015, May 15). *Microsoft study claims human attention span now lags behind goldfish.* Medical Xpress. https://medicalxpress.com/news/2015-05-microsoft-human-attention-span-lags.html

Chapter 3: The News

Brenan, M. (2019, September 26). Americans' Trust in Mass media Edges Down to 41%. Gallup. https://news.gallup.com/poll/267047/americans-trust-mass-media-edges-down.aspx

Bureau of Transportation Statistics. (2019). U.S. General Aviation Safety Data. United States Department of Transportation. https://www.bts.gov/content/us-general-aviationa-safety-data

Ecker, U.K.H., Lewandowsky, S., Chang, E.P., & Pillai, R. (2014). The Effects of Subtle Misinformation in News Headlines. *Journal of Experimental Psychology: Applied* 20(4): 323–335. https://doi.org/10.1037/xap0000028

Geiger, A.W. (2019, September 11). Key findings about the online news landscape in America. *FactTank: News in the Numbers.* Pew Research Center. https://www.pewresearch.org/fact-tank/2019/09/11/key-findings-about-the-online-news-landscape-in-america/

Haile, T. (2014, March 9). What You Think You Know About the Web is Wrong. *Time.* https://time.com/12933/what-you-think-you-know-about-the-web-is-wrong/

References

Kavanagh, J., Marcellino, W., Blake, J.S., Smith, S., Davenport, S., & Tebeka, M.G. (2019). News in a Digital Age: Comparing the Presentation of News Information over Time and Across Media Platforms. RAND Corporation. https://www.rand.org/pubs/research_reports/RR2960.html

Kobayashi, K., & Hsu, M. (2019). Common neural code for reward and information value. *Proceedings of the National Academy of Sciences* 116(26): 13061–13066. DOI: 10.1073/pnas.1820145116

Leetaru, K.H. (2011). Culturomics 2.0: Forecasting large-scale human behavior using global news media tone in time and space. *First Monday* 16(9). https://firstmonday.org/ojs/index.php/fm/article/view/3663/3040

National Highway Traffic Safety Administration (2019). Traffic Deaths Decreased in 2018, but Still 36,560 People Died. United States Department of Transportation. https://www.nhtsa.gov/traffic-deaths-2018

Pew Research Center Journalism and Media Staff. (2000, October 31). The Last Lap: Negative vs. Positive. Pew Research Center. https://www.journalism.org/2000/10/31/negative-vs-positive/

Soroush, V., Roy, D., & Aral, S. (2018). The spread of true and false news online. *Science* 359(6380): 1146–1151. DOI: 10.1126/science.aap9559

Trussler, M., & Soroka, S. (2014). Consumer Demand for Cynical and Negative News Frames. *International Journal of Press/Politics* 19(3): 360–379. https://doi.org/10.1177/1940161214524832

Tversky, A., & Kahneman, D. (1974). Judgment under Uncertainty: Heuristics and Biases. *Science* 185(4157): 1124–1131. DOI: 10.1126/science.185.4157.1124

Chapter 4: Instagram Worthy

Allianz Global Assistance. (2018, July 12). Millennials Most Like to Post Deceptive Vacation Photos to Make Social Media Followers Jealous. Alliance Travel. https://www.prnewswire.com/news-releases/millennials-most-likely-to-post-deceptive-vacation-photos-to-make-social-media-followers-jealous-300679940.html

Barasch, A., Diehl, K., Silverman, J., & Zauberman, G. (2017). Photographic Memory: The Effects of Volitional Photo Taking on Memory for Visual and Auditory Aspects of an Experience. *Psychological Science* 28(8): 1056–1066. https://doi.org/10.1177/0956797617694868

Henkel, L.A. (2014). Point-and-Shoot Memories: The Influence of Taking Photos on Memory for a Museum Tour. *Psychological Science* 25(2): 396–402. https://doi.org/10.1177/0956797613504438

Roudi, M. (2015, June 12). Norm Macdonald Last Stand Up on Letterman. Video. https://www.youtube.com/watch?v=mFjEvl43zYY&t=396s

Snowden, H. (2018). Some Millennials Aren't Enjoying their Vacations as much as Instagram Suggests. *Highsnobiety*. https://www.highsnobiety.com/p/millennials-social-media-oversell-vacation/

Storm, B.C., Stone, S.M., & Benjamin, A.S. (2017). Using the Internet to access information inflates future use of the Internet to access other information. *Memory* 25(6): 717–723, DOI: 10.1080/09658211.2016.1210171

Taylor & Francis. (2016, August 16). Cognitive offloading: How the Internet is increasingly taking over human memory. *ScienceDaily*. www.sciencedaily.com/releases/2016/08/160816085029.htm

Chapter 5: Who's the Pigeon Now?

Equals Four Media. (2017, December 11). *Fmr. Facebook Exec [Chamath Palihapitiya]: Social Media Ripping Apart Society, You are programmed.* Video. https://www.youtube.com/watch?v=d6e1riShmak

Eyal, N. (2013). *Hooked: How to Build Habit-Forming Products.* Penguin Group.

Schüll, N.D. (2012). *Addiction by Design: Machine Gambling in Las Vegas.* Princeton University Press.

Chapter 6: A Habit of Distraction

Duhigg, C. (2012). *The Power of Habit: Why We Do What We Do in Life and Business.* Random House Trade Paperbacks.

Flaxington, B.D. (2013). *Self-Talk for a Calmer You.* Adams Media. https://www.journals.uchicago.edu/doi/abs/10.1086/691462

Hiniker, A., Sungsoo, H, Kohno, T., & Kientz, J.A. 2016. MyTime: Designing and Evaluating an Intervention for Smartphone Non-Use. *Proceedings of the 2016 CHI Conference on Human Factors in Computing Systems* 4746–4757. DOI: https://doi.org/10.1145/2858036.2858403

Killingsworth, M.A., & Gilbert, D.T. (2010). A Wandering Mind is an Unhappy Mind. Supplemental material. *Science* 330, 932. DOI: 10.1126/science.1192439. https://wjh-www.harvard.edu/~dtg/KILLINGSWORTH%20&%20GILBERT%20(2010).pdf

Madore, K.P., Khazenzon, A.M., Backes, C.W., Jiang, J., Uncapher, M.R., Norcia, A.M., & Wagner, A.D. (2020). Memory failure predicted by attention lapsing and media multitasking. *Nature* 587, 87–91. https://doi.org/10.1038/s41586-020-2870-z

Michigan State University. (2018, September 26). Sleep research uncovers dire consequences to deprivation. *MSUToday*. https://msutoday.msu.edu/news/2018/sleep-research-uncovers-dire-consequences-to-deprivation/

Vogels, E.A., & Anderson, M. (2020, May 8). Dating and Relationships in the Digital Age. Pew Research Center. https://www.pewresearch.org/internet/2020/05/08/dating-and-relationships-in-the-digital-age/

Ward, A.F., Duke, K., Gneezy, A., & Bos, M.W. (2017). Brain Drain: The Mere Presence of One's Own Smartphone Reduces Available Cognitive Capacity. *Journal of the Association of Consumer Research* 2(2). https://doi.org/10.1086/691462

Wood, W. (2019). *Good Habits, Bad Habits: The Science of Making Positive Changes*. Farrar, Straus and Giroux.

Chapter 7: Tinder and I Are Registered on Amazon

Arikha, N. (2009). Up Close and Personal: The evolution of personal ads, from the newspaper to the social network. *Lapham's Quarterly*. https://www.laphamsquarterly.org/eros/close-and-personal

Center for Humane Technology. (n.d.). App Ratings. https://www.humanetech.com/app-ratings

D'Angelo, J.D., & Toma, C.L. (2017). There Are Plenty of Fish in the Sea: The Effects of Choice Overload and Reversibility on Online Daters' Satisfaction With Selected Partners. *Media Psychology* 20(1): 1–27. DOI: 10.1080/15213269.2015.1121827

Giaimo, C. (2016, September 30). Videocassette Dating Let Singles Fast-Forward to Love. *Atlas Obscura*. https://www.atlasobscura.com/articles/videocassette-dating-let-singles-fastforward-to-love

McGloin, R., & Denes, A. (2016). Too hot to trust: Examining the relationship between attractiveness, trustworthiness, and desire to date in online dating. *New Media & Society* 20. DOI: 10.1177/1461444816675440.

Sedgewick, J.R., Flath, M.E., & Elias, L.J. (2017). Presenting Your Best Self(ie): The Influence of Gender on Vertical Orientation of Selfies on Tinder. *Frontiers in Psychology* 8, 604. https://doi.org/10.3389/fpsyg.2017.00604

Strübel, J., & Petrie, T. (2017). Love me Tinder: Body image and psychosocial functioning among men and women. *Body Image* 21. DOI: 10.1016/j.bodyim.2017.02.006

Weigel, M. (2016). *Labor of Love: The Invention of Dating.* Farrar, Straus, and Giroux.

Chapter 8: Confirmation Bias

Baer, D. (2017, January 13). Kahneman: Your Cognitive Biases Act Like Optical Illusions. *The Cut.* https://www.thecut.com/2017/01/kahneman-biases-act-like-optical-illusions.html

Keegan, J. (2019, August 19). Blue Feed, Red Feed: See liberal Facebook and conservative Facebook, side by side. *Wall Street Journal.* https://graphics.wsj.com/blue-feed-red-feed/

Lord, C.G., Ross, L., & Lepper, M.R. (1979). Biased Assimilation and Attitude Polarization: The Effects of Prior Theories on Subsequently Considered Evidence. *Journal of Personality and Social Psychology* 37(11): 2098–2109. https://citeseerx.ist.psu.edu/viewdoc/download?doi=10.1.1.372.1743&rep=rep1&type=pdf

Mendel, R., Traut-Mattausch, E., Jonas, E., Leucht, S., Kane, J. M., Maino, K., Kissling, W., & Hamann, J. (2011). Confirmation bias: Why psychiatrists stick to wrong preliminary diagnoses. *Psychological Medicine* 41(12): 2651–2659. https://doi.org/10.1017/S0033291711000808

Chapter 9: Compassion Fatigue

American Psychological Association. (2019). Stress in America 2019. https://www.apa.org/news/press/releases/stress/2019/stress-america-2019.pdf

Guardian. (2019). Alan Kurdi: the latest news and comment on Alan Kurdi, the three-year-old Syrian boy who drowned in the Mediterranean Sea during the Syrian refugee crisis. Compilation of articles. https://www.theguardian.com/world/alan-kurdi

Mintz, L. (2017, January 11). Photo of dead Syrian boy boosts fundraising 100-fold: study. Reuters. https://www.reuters.com/article/us-europe-migrants-toddler/photo-of-dead-syrian-boy-boosts-fundraising-100-fold-study-idUSKBN14V2MH

Slovic, P., Västfjäll, D., Erlandsson, A., & Gregory, R. (2017). Ebb and flow of empathic response. *Proceedings of the National Academy of Sciences* 114(4): 640–644; DOI: 10.1073/pnas.1613977114

Thompson, R.R. (2018). *Psychological Implications of Indirect Media Exposure to Collective Traumas.* Doctoral dissertation, University of California, Irvine. eScholarship. https://escholarship.org/uc/item/86r7310w

Chapter 10: Too Much Information

Gorman, S.E. (2017). *Denying to the Grave: Why We Ignore the Facts That Will Save Us.* Oxford University Press.

Great Mirror. Wikipedia. https://en.wikipedia.org/wiki/Great_Mirror

Huettich, J. (2020, February 10). The ultimate guide to managing information overload. MindManager Blog. https://blog.mindmanager.com/blog/2020/02/202002the-ultimate-guide-to-managing-information-overload/

Stepper, J. (2016, October 22). Why Socrates thought writing was a bad idea. *Working Out Loud.* https://workingoutloud.com/blog/socrates-thought-writing-bad-idea

Chapter 11: FOMO

Bloom, L., & Bloom, C. (2004). *101 Things I Wish I Knew When I Got Married: Simple Lessons to Make Love Last.* New World Library.

Custard. (2016). Over three quarters of Brits say their social media page is a lie. Custard Online Marketing. https://www.custard.co.uk/over-three-quarters-of-brits-say-their-social-media-page-is-a-lie/

Hunt, M.G., Marx, R., Lipson, C., & Young, J. (2018). No More FOMO: Limiting Social Media Decreases Loneliness and Depression. *Journal of Social and Clinical Psychology* 37(10): 751–768. https://doi.org/10.1521/jscp.2018.37.10.751. https://guilford-journals.com/doi/pdf/10.1521/jscp.2018.37.10.751

Lexico. (2020). FOMO. Oxford English Dictionary. https://www.lexico.com/definition/fomo

Przybylski, A.K., Murayama, K., DeHaan, C.R., & Gladwell, V. (2013). Motivational, emotional, and behavioral correlates of fear of missing out. *Computers in Human Behavior* 29(4): 1841–1848. https://doi.org/10.1016/j.chb.2013.02.014

Vallerand, R. (2000). Deci and Ryan's Self-Determination Theory: A View from the Hierarchical Model of Intrinsic and Extrinsic Motivation. *Psychological Inquiry* 11(4): 312–318. http://www.jstor.org/stable/1449629

Chapter 12: Outrage Machine

Bartlett, R.C. (2019). *Aristotle's Art of Rhetoric.* University of Chicago Press.

Brady, W.J., Gantman, A.P., & Van Bavel, J.J. (2020). Attentional capture helps explain why moral and emotional content go viral. *Journal of Experimental Psychology: General* 149(4): 746–756. https://doi.org/10.1037/xge0000673

Brady, W.J., Wills, J.A., Jost, J.T., Tucker, J.A., & Van Bavel, J.J. (2017). Emotion shapes the diffusion of moralized content in social networks. *Proceedings of the National Academy of Sciences of the United States of America* 114(28): 7313–7318. https://doi.org/10.1073/pnas.1618923114

Kreider, T. (2009, July 14). Isn't It Outrageous? *New York Times.* https://opinionator.blogs.nytimes.com/2009/07/14/isnt-it-outrageous/

Jordan, J., Hoffman, M., Bloom, P., & Rand, D. (2016). Third-party punishment as a costly signal of trustworthiness. *Nature* 530, 473–476. https://doi.org/10.1038/nature16981

Sawaoka, T., & Monin, B. (2018). The Paradox of Viral Outrage. *Psychological Science* 29(10): 1665–1678. https://doi.org/10.1177/0956797618780658

Slate. (2014, December 17). The Year of Outrage. *Slate.* http://
www.slate.com/articles/life/culturebox/2014/12/the_year_of_
outrage_2014_everything_you_were_angry_about_on_social_
media.html

Stevens, H. R., Graham, P. L., Beggs, P. J., & Hanigan, I. C. (2020). In
Cold Weather We Bark, But in Hot Weather We Bite: Patterns in
Social Media Anger, Aggressive Behavior, and Temperature. *Envi-
ronment and Behavior.* https://doi.org/10.1177/0013916520937455

Twenge, J.M., & Campbell, W.K. (2009). *The narcissism epidemic.* Atria
Paperback.

Chapter 13: Tribalism

Cialdini, R., Borden, R., Thorne, A., Walker, M., Freeman, S., &
Sloan, L. (1976). Basking in Reflected Glory: Three (Football)
Field Studies. *Journal of Personality and Social Psychology* 34(3): 366–
375. DOI: 10.1037/0022-3514.34.3.366

Ditto, P. H., Liu, B. S., Clark, C. J., Wojcik, S. P., Chen, E. E., Grady,
R. H., Celniker, J. B., & Zinger, J. F. (2019). At Least Bias Is Bipar-
tisan: A Meta-Analytic Comparison of Partisan Bias in Liberals and
Conservatives. *Perspectives on Psychological Science* 14(2): 273–291.
https://doi.org/10.1177/1745691617746796

Khaldun, I. (1377). *The Muqaddimah.* Translated by Franz Rosenthal.
https://asadullahali.files.wordpress.com/2012/10/ibn_khaldun-
al_muqaddimah.pdf

Mirer, M., Duncan, M., & Wagner, M. (2018). Taking it from the team:
Assessments of bias and credibility in team-operated sports media.
Newspaper Research Journal 39(4). DOI: 10.1177/0739532918806890

Packer, G. (2018, October 13). A new report offers insights into tribalism in the age of Trump. *New Yorker.* https://www.newyorker
.com/news/daily-comment/a-new-report-offers-insights-into-
tribalism-in-the-age-of-trump

Pew Research Center. (2019, October 10). Partisan Antipathy: How
partisans view each other. https://www.pewresearch.org/politics/
2019/10/10/how-partisans-view-each-other/

Pew Research Center. (2019, October 10). Partisan Antipathy:
More Intense, More Personal. https://www.pewresearch.org/
politics/2019/10/10/partisan-antipathy-more-intense-more-
personal/

University of Minnesota. (2009, March 24). Fear Or Romance Could Make You Change Your Mind, Study Finds. *ScienceDaily*. www.sciencedaily.com/releases/2009/03/090323134313.htm

Warren, L. (2013, November 30). *Cheering for Clothes?* Minor League Ball. https://www.minorleagueball.com/2013/11/30/5159958/cheering-for-clothes

Chapter 14: Instant Gratification

Dar, R. Rosen-Korakin, N., Shapira, O., Gottlieb, Y., Frenk, H. (2010). The craving to smoke in flight attendants: Relations with smoking deprivation, anticipation of smoking, and actual smoking. *Journal of Abnormal Psychology* 119(1): 248–253.

Fifth Third Bank. (2015, January 27). Ninety-Six Percent of Americans Are So Impatient They Knowingly Consume Hot Food or Beverages That Burn Their Mouths, Finds Fifth Third Bank Survey. Fifth Third Bancorp. https://www.prnewswire.com/news-releases/ninety-six-percent-of-americans-are-so-impatient-they-knowingly-consume-hot-food-or-beverages-that-burn-their-mouths-finds-fifth-third-bank-survey-300026261.html

Hadar, A., Hadas, I., Lazarovits, A., Alyagon, U., Eliraz, D., & Zangen, A. (2017). Answering the missed call: Initial exploration of cognitive and electrophysiological changes associated with smartphone use and abuse. *PLOS ONE* 12(7). https://doi.org/10.1371/journal.pone.0180094

Kidd, C., Palmeri, H., & Aslin, R.N. (2013). Rational snacking: Young children's decision-making on the marshmallow task is moderated by beliefs about environmental reliability. *Cognition* 126(1): 109–114. https://doi.org/10.1016/j.cognition.2012.08.004

Krishnan, S.S., & Sitaraman, R.K. (2012). Video Stream Quality Impacts Viewer Behavior: Inferring Causality Using Quasi-Experimental Designs. *Proceedings of the ACM Internet Measurement Conference*. https://people.cs.umass.edu/~ramesh/Site/HOME_files/imc208-krishnan.pdf

Nielsen Norman Group. (2020). How People Read Online: The Eyetracking Evidence (2nd ed.). https://www.nngroup.com/reports/how-people-read-web-eyetracking-evidence/

Princeton University. (2004, October 14). Study: Brain battles itself over short-term rewards, long-term goals. Press release. https://pr.princeton.edu/news/04/q4/1014-brain.htm

Chapter 15: Loneliness

Chopik, W.J. (2016). The Benefits of Social Technology Use Among Older Adults Are Mediated by Reduced Loneliness. *Cyberpsychology, Behavior, and Social Networking* 19(9): 551–556. http://doi.org/10.1089/cyber.2016.0151

Cigna. (2020). Loneliness and the Workplace. https://www.cigna.com/static/www-cigna-com/docs/about-us/newsroom/studies-and-reports/combatting-loneliness/cigna-2020-loneliness-factsheet.pdf

Matthews, G.A., Nieh, E.H., Vander Weele, C.M., Halbert, S.A., Pradhan, R.V., Yosafat, A.S., Glober, G.F., Izadmehr, E.M., Thomas, R.E., Lacy, G.D., Wildes, C.P., Ungless, M.A., & Tye, K.M. (2016). Dorsal Raphe Dopamine Neurons Represent the Experience of Social Isolation. *Cell* 164(4): 617–631. https://doi.org/10.1016/j.cell.2015.12.040

Murthy, V.H. (2020). *Together: The Healing Power of Human Connection in a Sometimes Lonely World.* HarperCollins Publishers.

Steiner-Adair, C. (2014). *The Big Disconnect: Protecting Childhood and Family Relationships in the Digital Age.* HarperCollins Publishers.

Yang, C. (2016). Instagram Use, Loneliness, and Social Comparison Orientation: Interact and Browse on Social Media, But Don't Compare. *CyberPsychology, Behavior, and Social Networking* 19(12): 703–708. DOI: 10.1089/cyber.2016.0201

Chapter 16: Choice

Botti, S., & Inesi, M.E. (2011). Power and Choice: A Compensatory Theory of Control. Abstract. *NA: Advances in Consumer Research* 38, eds. Darren W. Dahl, Gita V. Johar, and Stijn M.J. van Osselaer (Eds.), Duluth, MN: Association for Consumer Research. https://www.acrwebsite.org/volumes/15894/volumes/v38/NA-38

Chou, H.G., Edge, N. (2012). "They Are Happier and Having Better Lives than I Am": The Impact of Using Facebook on Perceptions of Others' Lives. *Cyberpsychology, Behavior, and Social Networking* 15(2). DOI: 10.1089/cyber.2011.0324

Financial Express Online. (2019, November 21). Starbucks menu has over 80,000 coffees; will take three human lifetimes to try them all. https://www.financialexpress.com/industry/starbucks-menu-has-over-80000-coffees-will-take-three-human-lifetimes-to-try-them-all/1771490/

Hedges, K. (2017). *The Inspiration Code: How the Best Leaders Energize People Every Day.* American Management Association.

Iyengar, S.S., & Lepper, M.R. (2001). When Choice is Demotivating: Can One Desire Too Much of a Good Thing? *Journal of Personality and Social Psychology.* DOI: 10.1037/0022-3514.79.6.995

Langer, E.J., & Rodin, J. (1976). The effects of choice and enhanced personal responsibility for the aged: A field experiment in an institutional setting. *Journal of Personality and Social Psychology* 34(2): 191–198. https://doi.org/10.1037/0022-3514.34.2.191

Rodin, J., & Langer, E.J. (1977). Long-term effects of a control-relevant intervention with the institutionalized aged. *Journal of Personality and Social Psychology* 35(12): 897–902. https://doi.org/10.1037/0022-3514.35.12.897

Shwartz, B. (2004). *The Paradox of Choice: Why More Is Less. How the Culture of Abundance Robs Us of Satisfaction.* HarperCollins Publishers.

Simon, H.A. (1978). Rationality as Process and as Product of Thought. *American Economic Review* 68(2): 1–16. https://www.jstor.org/stable/1816653?seq=1

Chapter 17: Impulse Buying

Merzer, M. (2014, November 24). Survey: 3 in 4 Americans make impulse purchases. CreditCards.com https://www.creditcards.com/credit-card-news/impulse-purchase-survey/

O'Brien, S. (2018, February 23). Consumers Cough Up $5,400 a Year on Impulse Purchases. CNBC.com. https://www.cnbc.com/2018/02/23/consumers-cough-up-5400-a-year-on-impulse-purchases.html.

Pychyl, T.A. (2013). *Solving the Procrastination Puzzle: A Concise Guide to Strategies for Change.* Penguin Group.

Richards, C. (2015, August 3). What Is Our Attention Really Worth? *New York Times.* https://www.nytimes.com/2015/08/03/your-money/what-is-our-attention-really-worth.html

Williams, J. (2018). *Stand Out of Our Light: Freedom and Resistance in the Attention Economy.* Cambridge University Press.

Chapter 18: Porn

Castleman, M. (2009, April 27). Does Pornography Cause Social Harm? *Psychology Today*. https://www.psychologytoday.com/us/blog/all-about-sex/200904/does-pornography-cause-social-harm

FindLaw Attorney Writers. (2016, April 26). Movie Day at the Supreme Court or "I Know It When I See It": A History of the Definition of Obscenity. *FindLaw for Legal Professionals*. https://corporate.findlaw.com/litigation-disputes/movie-day-at-the-supreme-court-or-i-know-it-when-i-see-it-a.html

Perry, S.L. (2020, November). Does Low-Cost Sexual Gratification Make Men Less Eager to Marry? *Archives of Sexual Behavior* 49(3): 3013–3026. DOI: 10.1007/s10508-020-01793-w

Perry, S.L., & Schleifer, C. (2018). Till Porn Do Us Part? A Longitudinal Examination of Pornography Use and Divorce. *Journal of Sex Research* 55(3): 284–296. https://doi.org/10.1080/00224499.2017.1317709

Pornhub. (2019, December 11). Pornhub 2019 Year in Review. https://www.pornhub.com/insights/2019-year-in-review

Chapter 19: Publisher or Platform?

Baum, M.A., Ognyanova, K., Chwe, H., Quintana, A., Perlis, R.H., Lazer, D., Druckman, J., Santillana, M., Lin, J., Della Volpe, J., Simonson, M., & Green, J. (2020, September 23). The State of the Nation: A 50-State COVID-19 Survey. Report #14: Misinformation and vaccine acceptance. COVID-19 Consortium for Understanding the Public's Policy Preference Across States. https://news.northeastern.edu/wp-content/uploads/2020/09/COVID19-CONSORTIUM-REPORT-14-MISINFO-SEP-2020-2.pdf

Fonrouge, G. (2020, October 28). What is Section 230 and why was it created? *New York Post*. https://nypost.com/article/what-is-section-230-and-why-was-it-created/

Harwell, D. (2019, May 24). Fake Pelosi videos, slowed to make her appear drunk, spread across social media. *Washington Post*. https://www.washingtonpost.com/technology/2019/05/23/faked-pelosi-videos-slowed-make-her-appear-drunk-spread-across-social-media/

Office of U.S. Senator Michael Bennet. 2020, February 24). Bennet Responds to Facebook Calling for More Responsibility for its

Damages to Democratic Values Around the World. Press release. https://www.bennet.senate.gov/public/index.cfm/2020/2/bennet-responds-to-facebook-calling-for-more-responsibility-for-its-damage-to-democratic-values-around-the-world

Oxford Internet Institute. (2019, September 26). Use of social media to manipulate public opinion now a global problem, says new report. Press release. University of Oxford. https://www.oii.ox.ac.uk/news/releases/use-of-social-media-to-manipulate-public-opinion-now-a-global-problem-says-new-report

U.S. Department of Justice. (2020, September 23). Department of Justice's Review of Section 230 of the Communications Decency Act of 1996. https://www.justice.gov/ag/department-justice-s-review-section-230-communications-decency-act-1996

White House. (2020, May 28). Executive Order on Preventing Online Censorship. https://www.whitehouse.gov/presidential-actions/executive-order-preventing-online-censorship/

Chapter 20: Algorithms

Fry, H. (2018). *Hello World: Being Human in the Age of Algorithms*. W.W. Norton & Company.

Jagadish, H.V. (2015, November 20). The Reality of Crime-Fighting Algorithms. *Slate*. https://slate.com/technology/2015/11/using-data-science-for-predictive-policing-has-serious-civil-liberties-drawbacks.html

Ranie, L., & Anderson, J. (2017, February 8). Code-Dependent: Pros and Cons of the Algorithm Age. Theme 7: The need grows for algorithmic literacy, transparency and oversight. Pew Research Center. https://www.pewresearch.org/internet/2017/02/08/theme-7-the-need-grows-for-algorithmic-literacy-transparency-and-oversight/

Smith, A. (2018, November 16). Public Attitudes Toward Computer Algorithms. 1. Attitudes toward algorithmic decision-making. Pew Research Center. https://www.pewresearch.org/internet/2018/11/16/attitudes-toward-algorithmic-decision-making/

Thompson, N. (2018, October 4). When Tech Knows You Better Than You Know Yourself. *Wired*. https://www.wired.com/story/artificial-intelligence-yuval-noah-harari-tristan-harris/

Tutt, A. (2016). An FDA for Algorithms. *Administrative Law Review* 83. http://dx.doi.org/10.2139/ssrn.2747994

Index

101 Things I Wish I Knew When I Got Married (Bloom), 90

A

Abortion, charged issue, 65–66
Addiction by Design (Dow Schüll), 45
Advertising revenue, attraction, 14–15
Algorithms
  creation, 164
  harm, reduction, 163
  impact, 106
  net-positive effect, 163–164
  oversight, 164–165
  predictions, inaccuracy, 159
  regulation/transparency, requirement, 164
  rules, impact, 162
  usage, 4–5, 96–97, 100, 157–164
Alone Togetherness (Turkle), 8
Amazon, users, 55
Amygdala
  hijack, curbing, 141
  impact, 26
  trigger, 88
Anger, channeling, 102
Anxiety
  channeling, 102
  conversion, 170
  experience, 78
  study, 90
AOL, initiation, 43–44

Applications (apps), deletion, 169–170
Aristotle, 28, 95, 129
Artificial intelligence (AI)
  recommendations, importance, 160
Attention, 11
  adjustment, 51
  budget, creation, 140–142
  capture, 112–113
  competition, technology (impact), 137–138
  control, ability, 48–49
  defining, 13–16
  description, 13–14
  devotion, example, 12
  drawing/keeping, 21–23
  economy, basis, 6
  fight, 137–140
  focus, 2–3, 137, 140
    difficulty, 16–17
  management, 141
  maximization, 161
  maximum, 14
  online attention, gaining (difficulty), 100
  prioritization, 12
  push, 75–76
  redirection, 137
  resource, 17–28, 142
  reward, 44–45
  scarcity, 5–7, 15

Attention (*Continued*)
  scenarios, 12
  shift, 137
  spans, examination, 16–17
  switching, 51
  technology, relationship, 16–17
  term, meaning, 13
  value, realization, 172
  zero-sum game, 6, 49
Attention deficit hyperactivity
    disorder (ADHD),
    diagnosis, 17
Authenticity, importance, 174
Autonomy, 90, 92
Awareness, importance, 53–54

B
Barasch, Alixandra, 33, 34, 37
Basking in reflected glory
    (BIRG), 105
Behavior
  motivation, 40, 42
  tracking, 140–141
Belonging, sense, 125
Bennet, Michael, 153–154
Biases, 152
  addressing, 69–70
  challenge, 171
  concerns, 159
  confirmation bias, 63–67, 171
  implicit bias, 105, 109
  input bias, 162
  partisan bias, 107
  representation, 159
  support, sources (impact), 67–71
Bickert, Monika, 152
Big Disconnect, The (Steiner-Adair),
    123
Binge-watching, 113
Bloom, Linda/Charlie, 59, 90, 93

"Blue Feed, Red Feed" (Wall Street
    Journal), 67–68
Bragbook, 88
Brain
  chess analogy, 161–162
  dump, 85
  fog, 173–174
  pathways, reinforcement, 113
Breaking news, 95, 168
  phrase, response, 23–24
Broadcast television news, analysis,
    22–23
Browsing, Facebook tracking, 162
Budget
  creation, 140–141
  usage, 136
Buffett, Warren, 63
Buridan, Jean, 130
Buridan's ass, 129–130

C
Cable news
  analysis, 22–23
  attention/ratings, 23
  consumption habit,
    recognition, 117
  importance, increase, 20
  watching, 101–102
Cameras, usage, 33–34
Campbell, Keith, 98, 99, 102
Campbell, Kelly, 60–61
Candid photos, usage, 34
Castleman, Michael, 147–148
Catfishing, usage, 59
Chabris, Chris, 13
Choice, 127
  control, combination, 128
  filtration, 171
  freedom, 128
  jam selection (study), 129

overload, 129–132
  combatting, 133–134
  power, relationship, 128
Chopik, William, 121–122
Clickbaits
  headlines, 25–26, 168
  usage, 21
Click tracking, 25
Climate change, charged issue,
  65–66
Close-mindedness, feeling, 108
Cognitive capacity
  drain, 53
  limitation, 6–7
  usage, increase, 50
Cognitive decline, loneliness
  (impact), 120
Cognitive fatigue, 84
Cognitive offloading, 32
Cognitive override, performing,
  101–102
Commitment, resistance,
  59–60
Communications Act, Section 230,
  150–154
Compassion fatigue, 73
  emotional/physical
    exhaustion, 74
  media contribution, 76–77
  social problems, relationship,
    76–77
  symptoms, 74
Compassion, power, 77–78
Competence, 92
Confirmation bias, 9, 19–20,
  63, 170
  creation, 152–153
  effects, countering, 69
  elements, 25–26
  impact, 23

knowledge, 65–67
  tendency, 64
Connecting
  instant messaging, usage, 8
  social media, usage, 9–10
Connections, 92
  in-person connections, barriers
    (creation), 122
  multitude, impact, 124–125
Conspiracy theories, 152
  popularity, 160–161
  space, 110
Contact, elimination, 63–64
Control, choice (combination), 128
Conversation, increase, 173
Cook, Beano, 9
Couples, pornography (problems),
  145–146, 148
COVID-19 pandemic
  information sources/beliefs,
    152–153
  medical collaborations, 9
Cronkite, Walter, 20

D
Data
  broker, personal information
    sale, 163
  creation, 4–5
  evaluation, 69
  filtering, 65
Dating. *See* Online dating
Decisions, 127
  elimination, 45
  example, 6–7
  sources, locating (impact), 134
Denying to the Grave (Gorman), 84
Depression, 90
  loneliness, impact, 120–121
Digital environment, currency, 22

Discourse, limitation, 66
Discussion boards, back and forth, 28
Distractions, 124
  active management, 17
  elimination, 50
  emotional distractions,
    source, 49
  external distractions, 53
  habit, 47
    breaking, 52–54
  ignoring, stress, 16
  internal distractions, 49–52
  sensory distractions, 48–49
  short-term goals/long-term goals,
    relationship, 138–139
  ubiquity, 47–48
  waste, 52
Ditto, Peter, 107
Divorce (increase), pornography
    (impact), 146
Dogma, criticism, 109
Dopamine, 53, 168
  fast, 173
  fun feeling, 40
  impact, 23–24, 42–43
  loop, 37
  receiving, 170
Dorsal raphe nucleus, activation, 121
Downtime, smartphone (usage), 52
Dow Schüll, Natasha, 45
Duhigg, Charles, 53
Duncan, Megan A., 106, 109

E
Echo chambers, 4, 70–71, 161, 170
  creation, 36, 152–153
  effects, countering, 69
  formation, 108
  impact, 66
  usage, 68–69

Electronic engagement,
  perception, 123
Elements of Journalism, The (Kovach/
  Rosenstiel), 19
Emails
  attention, example, 2
  overload, 173–174
  prioritization, example, 79–80
  push notifications, impact,
    17–18
Emotional distractions, source, 49
Emotional loneliness, 121
Emotional self-control, power, 70
Emotions
  impact, 107
  present, impact, 115–116
Empathy, 75–77
  absence, 75
  power, 70–71
Empowerment, 172–174
  sense, 125
Environment, management, 116
Events, probability (estimation), 27
Existential loneliness, 121
Experiences
  devotion, attention, 36–37
  echo chamber, creation, 36
  reconfiguration, 36
  selection, 37–38
External transactions,
  management, 53
External triggers, impact, 43
Extrinsic motivation, 92
Eyal, Nir, 17, 43

F
Facebook
  development, 44
  friends, 67
    loneliness, presence, 121–126

impact, 132–133
legal protection, 151
life, exaggeration, 89
maximizer usage, 132–133
misuse, growth, 153–154
moderators, settlement, 76–77
pictures (photos), uploading,
    32–33
posts, 43, 98, 102
profiles, 70–71
time, usage, 140
tracking, 162
users, number, 5
Facebook content
discovery, 43
responsibility, 152
user knowledge, 158
Face-to-face interactions,
    avoidance, 99
Fact-based questions
    (Pew study), 25
Facts, editing/rechecking
    (decrease), 168
False news, spread, 24
Fear of missing out (FOMO),
    9, 61, 87
exit/freedom, 93–94
feelings, 171
impact, 124–125
measure, 91–92
social media, impact, 88–92
Feedback, 79–80
loops, 22
Fight or flight response, 88
amygdala, impact, 26
Figley, Charles, 75
Filter bubbles
effects, countering, 69
elements, 25–26
existence, 27–28

exit, 101–102, 170
usage, 68–69
Financial decision-making,
    136, 138
First Amendment, free speech
    rights, 150
First impression, 64
Fixed-ratio reinforcement
    schedule, 42
Flaxington, Beverly, 50–51, 53
Focus
attention, focus, 2–3, 137
difficulty, 5, 16–17
problem, 14
shift, 11–12
Free expression, tech company
    promotion, 151–152
Free will, reward/punishment
    (relationship), 40–41
Freud, Sigmund, 114
Friction, opportunities
    (creation), 53
Friends, connections, 4
Fry, Hannah, 163

G
Gamblers, brain scans (analysis), 24
Gettysburg Address, delivery
    (question), 21
Gilbert, Daniel, 49
Goals. *See* Long-term goals;
    Short-term goals
conversion, 116
determination, 7
meeting, 9–10, 139–140
Goldhaber, Michael, 15
Goldman, Eric, 151, 154, 155
Good Habits, Bad Habits
    (Wood), 52
Gorman, Sara, 84–85

Gratification. *See* Instant
    gratification
    delay, 114–115
Great Mirror, The (Vincent of
    Beauvais), 82–83
Griffin, Michael, 20, 22, 29,
    97, 99
Grindr, destination, 61
Griskevicius, Vladas, 107
Gun control, charged issue,
    65–66

H
Habit
    impact, 51–52
    recognition, 117
Harris, Tristan, 161–162
Hate speech, limitation, 154
Headline fatigue, 20
Headlines, news (relationship), 21
Heart disease (increase), loneliness
    (impact), 120
Hedges, Kristi, 131, 133–134
Hello World (Fry), 163
Henkel, Linda, 33
Hershfield, Hal, 113
HIV/AIDS, 73–74
Homophily, presence, 67
Hooked (Eyal), 43
Hunt, Melissa, 90

I
Impatience (Fifth Third Bank
    survey), 112
Implicit bias, 105, 109
Impulse buying, 135
Impulse purchases, consumer
    spending, 136
Impulsivity, 112–114
Indistractable (Eyal), 17

Information
    anticipation, brain activation, 24
    cherry-picking, 64
    comprehension, limitation, 5
    displacement, interruptions
        (impact), 15–16
    entry, 3–4
    exposure, 167
        impact, 81
        tiredness, 101–102
    feeling, regaining, 167
    filtering, 65
    instantaneousness, 112
    management, 83–85
    media sources, 25
    overload, 20, 79–83
        acceptance, 81–82
        symptoms, 83
    quality/reliability, 22
    receiving, 80
        speed, increase, 83
    search, ability, 67–68
    selectivity/prioritization,
        83–85
    silos, 22
    sources, 80
        attention (push), 75–76
        blocking, 108
    tweeting/retweeting, 24
    ubiquity, 80
Information age, 1, 67, 124
    by-products, 8–10
    choices, 131–132
    pitfalls, avoidance, 169
    research ability, 132
In-person connections, barriers
    (creation), 122
Input bias, 162
Inspiration Code, The (Hedges),
    131

Instagram, 1, 31, 43
  activities, study, 13–124
Instant gratification, 111
  fueling, 117
  impulsivity, 112–114
Instant messages, overload,
    173–174
Instant messaging, impact, 126
Internal distractions, 49–52
  management, 53
Internal responses, 23–24
Internal triggers, impact, 17, 43
Internet
  content
    characterization, 149–150
    platform responsibilities, 152
  future, 155–156
  provider/user, publisher/
    platform interpretation, 149–
    150
  Section 230 (Communications
    Act), 150–154
  users, content knowledge, 158
Interruptions, impact, 15–16
Intrinsic motivation, 92
Intrinsic rewards, 39–40
Intrusions, ignoring, 48–49
Intuition, power, 133–134
Invisible Gorilla experiment,
    13–14
Issues, confirmation bias, 65–66

J
Jagadish, H.V., 159
James, William, 13, 14
Jordan, Jillian, 100
Journalism
  online journalism, analysis,
    22–23
  transparency, 29

K
Kahneman, Daniel, 27, 64
Kidd, Celeste, 115
Killingsworth, Matthew, 49
Kinnick, Katherine, 76
Kovach, Bill, 19
Kurdi, Alan (photo), 77

L
Labor of Love (Weigel), 55
Lankes, David, 163
Leetaru, Kalev, 26
Life
  deceleration, practice, 93
  exaggeration, 89
  unfairness, Facebook (impact),
    132–133
Lincoln, Abraham (honesty
    discussion), 21
Loneliness, 119
  addressing, 125
  connectedness, contrast, 4
  defining, 120
  feelings, experience,
    124–125
  presence, 121–126
  sense, feeling, 120–121
  solitude, contrast,
    120–121
  study, 90
  types, 121
Long-term gain, short-term
    rewards, 52
Long-term goals
  assistance, 45–46
  distraction, relationship,
    138–139
  meeting, 9–10
Long-term reward, uncertainty, 115
Ludden, David, 145

M

Machine learning, development, 162

Marriage (research), 146

Marshmallow experiment, 52–53, 115

Mate selection, 59–61
commitment, resistance, 59–60
options, 60
validation, hope, 61

Maximization Scale, self-rating, 130–131

Maximizers, 129, 171
Amazon, impact, 131–132
mate meeting, 60
role, 133

McCarley, Jason, 13, 15

Media. *See* Social media
multitasking, 51
public confidence, erosion, 28
public distrust, 27–28

Media and Community (Griffin), 20, 97

Mesolimbic pathway (reward pathway), 40

Messaging, risk, 56–57

Metacognitive skills, usage, 141

Money Talk (bulletin board), 149

Moral outrage, problems, 100–101

Morrison, Helen, 55

Motivation
action, impact, 141
reinforcement, 42–43

Muench, Fred, 45, 46

Multitasking
avoidance, 84
belief, 169

Murthy, Vivek, 125

N

Narcissism, social media (impact), 98–99

Negative news, exposure regularity, 27

News
24-hour cycle, 29
attention, continuation, 23–28
breaking news, 23–24, 95
cable news, importance (increase), 20
events, influence, 26
exposure, tiredness, 101–102
false news, spread, 24
headlines
relationship, 21
replacement, 19–20
ignoring, 6
impact, 76
landscape, challenges, 29
listening, example, 1–2
negative news, exposure regularity, 27
negative responses, 97–101
outlets, distrust, 27–28
self-editor role, 28–29
sensationalism, 9
sources, 20, 66, 97
television news, sourcing, 20
threat, 75

Newspapers, analysis, 22–23

News, sources, 19

Noise
impact, 16
reduction, results, 16

Novelty, impact, 24

O

Objectification, 59

OKCupid, destination, 61

Online attention, gaining
(difficulty), 100
Online censorship, prevention
(Executive Order), 154
Online dating, 59–61
apps, 56, 60
catfishing, usage, 59
choices, 60–61
commitment, resistance, 59–60
industry, profit, 56
objectification, 59
participation, 58
user rejection, 58–59
Online journalism, analysis, 22–23
Operant conditioning, 40–41
Opinions
impact, 168
opinion statements, labeling,
22–23
protection, 170
vindication, innate desire, 19–20
Options, consideration
(importance), 128–133
Outcome measures, study, 90
Outrage, 9
culture, defining, 96
feeling, 97–98
machine, 95
moral outrage, problems,
100–101
spread, 99

P
Packer, George, 104
Paliphapitiya, Chamath, 43–44
Paradox of Choice, The (Schwartz),
130
Partisan bias, 107
Partisan politics, meaning, 106
Partisanship, 28, 106

Partners, distraction, 48
Patient diagnosis, confirmation bias
(impact), 65
Patriotism, absence (feeling), 108
Pelosi, Nancy (video alteration),
151–152
Perry, Samuel, 145
Persistence, 52
Perspective, sharing, 168
Petrie, Trent, 58
Pettiness, 138–139
Phones. *See* Smartphones
Phubbing, 14, 122, 126
Pictures (photos)
candid photos, usage, 34
location identification, 33–34
posting, 34–38
profile pictures, resemblance,
57–59
sharing, 34
value, 57–58
Pleasure principle, 114
Polarization
approach, 109–110
creation, 66
increase, 170–171
Political partisanship, 106
Political perspectives, source, 63
Politics
partisan politics, meaning, 106
tribalism, 104
Pornhub, visits/uploads, 144
Pornography, 143
availability, 147
consumption, 144–147
demand, reasons, 144–145
imagination, absence,
146–147
problems, 145–146
quality, decision, 147–148

Pornography (*Continued*)
  sexual violence, correlation
    (absence), 147–148
  urges, satisfaction, 112
  usage (research), 146
Posts, creation, 44–45
Post-traumatic stress disorder
  (PTSD), 77
Power, choice (relationship), 128
Power of Habit, The (Duhigg), 53
Predictive policing, usage,
  158–159
Prejudices, compensation, 109
Principles of Psychology (James), 13
Procrastination, 141
Products, Amazon
  recommendations, 158
Profile pictures, resemblance,
  57–59
Profits, maximization, 164
Project Pigeon, 41
Prudence, 138–139
Przybylski, Andrew, 91
Public trust, erosion, 28
Punishments, rewards
  (relationship), 40–41
Push notification, 3
  impact, 17–18
  limitation, 169
  usage, 43
Pychyl, Tim, 139, 141

R
Radicalization, echo chambers
  (impact), 66
Real-life interactions, advantage,
  133
Reflection
  importance, 169–172
  power, 45–46

process, 46
ROI assessment, 54
Relationships
  strengthening, technology
    (usage), 122
  weakening, 125–126
Research ability, technology
  (impact), 132
Response, control (focus), 28
Return on investment (ROI),
  assessment, 54
Rewards, 39
  consideration, 116
  fixed-ratio reinforcement
    schedule, 42
  free will, relationship, 40–41
  motivation, 39–40
  pathway (mesolimbic
    pathway), 40
  short-term reward, social media
    (usage), 45–46
  study, fMRI (usage), 113–114
  uncertainty, 115–117
  value, 45–46
  variable rewards schedule,
    42–43
Richards, Carl, 140
Risk tolerance levels, variance,
  115–117
Rooney, Andy, 135
Rosenstiel, Tom, 19

S
Satisficers, internal threshold,
  128–129
Satisficing, coinage, 128–129
Scandals, vividness, 3
Schwartz, Barry, 130, 132
Screen-free time, 53
Screen time, average, 3, 8–9

Search engines
  algorithms, usage, 158
  democratic accountability, 164
Section 230 (Communications
    Act), 150–154
  FTC reinterpretation, requests,
    154
  repair, 155
Sedgewick, Jennifer, 57
Self-control, exhibition, 52
Self-determination theory, focus, 92
Self-discipline, 7
Self-esteem/self-acceptance, study,
    90
Self-presentation theory, 57–58
Self-promotion, desire, 90–91
Self-rating, 130–131
Self-regulation, usage, 139–140
Self-talk, engagement, 50–51
Self-Talk for a Calmer You
    (Flaxington), 50
Self-worth, 58
  measurement, 61
Sensationalism, 28
  dressing, 20
  impact, 168
  news, origin, 9
  protection, 170
  story factors, contrast, 21
Sensory distractions, 48–49
Sentiment mining, usage, 26
Shared experiences, 4
Short-term gain, 141–142
Short-term goals
  distraction, relationship, 138–139
  meeting, 9–10
Short-term rewards, 52
  social media, usage, 45–46
Simon, Herbert, 6, 128, 169
Simons, Daniel, 13

Sitaraman, Ramesh, 112
Site, publisher platform
    determination (analogy), 153
Skinner box, usage, 41, 45
Skinner, Burrhus Frederick, 40–41
Slot machines, reward example, 42
Smartphones
  alerts, active management, 17–18
  cameras, usage, 33–34
  checking, 3
  distractions, 124
  popularity, rise, 32
  presence, impact, 49–50
  relationship, 46
  usage, 14, 138
    avoidance, 173
  users, comparison, 112
Smoking deprivation, effects
    (study), 114
Social identity, impact, 107
Social loneliness, 121
Social media
  attachment, 41–45
  attention, devotion, 7
  back and forth, engagement, 28
  challenge, 89–90
  communication outlet, 94
  connections, 119–120
  content, 67–68
    production, 37–38
  distractions, 124
  engagement, 4, 8, 42–43,
    96–97
  experience, traction, 35–36
  extension, 56
  homophily, presence, 67
  impact, 88, 98–99
  internal triggers, impact, 17
  invention, 66–67
  novelty, impact, 24

Social media (*Continued*)
  photos
    posting, 37
  pictures (photos)
    sharing, 34–36
  posting/retweeting, 4
  posts, deception, 88–89
  scrolling, 51–52
  services, legal protection, 151
  sharing, purpose, 34–35
  variable rewards schedule,
    42–43
Social perspectives, source, 63
Social problems, compassion
  fatigue (relationship),
  76–77
Social status, conveyance, 24
Social support, study, 90
Solitude, loneliness (contrast),
  120–121
Solving the Procrastination Puzzle
  (Pychyl), 139
Spending, monitoring,
  140–141
Spivey, Michael, 105, 108
Stand Out of Our Light (Williams),
  138
Steiner-Adair, Catherine, 123,
  125–126
Stewart, Potter, 144
Storm, Benjamin, 32
Stosny, Steven, 28
Stress
  impact, 16
  news, impact, 76
Strubel, Jessica, 58, 61
Student performance, noise
  reduction (result), 16
Success, transference, 105
Sundar, Shyam, 21, 24, 26, 28

Survival, amygdala (impact), 26
Syrian refugee crisis
  (Kurdi photo), 77

T
Technology
  abandonment, 173
  attention, relationship, 16–17
  benefits, study, 121–122
  engagement, 70
  impact, 113, 137–138
  research ability, 132
  utilization, 173–174
Television news, sourcing, 20
Texting
  calling, alternative, 170
  example, 14–15
  limitation, 53
  transactional nature, 126
Text message, receiving, 47
Thinking, content, 49–52
Threats, impact, 96–97
Tinder, 132
  destination, 61
  options, 59–60
  usage, 56
  users, 55
Together (Murthy), 125
Tragedies
  compassion, 78
  vividness, 3
Tribalism, 9, 103, 170
  ease, 108
  impact, 105, 108–109
Tribes
  comparison, 104–107
  divisions, cessation, 108–110
Trump, Donald (social media ban),
  154
Trustworthiness, gain, 100

Turkle, Sherry, 8
Tutt, Andrew, 158, 161, 164
Tversky, Amos, 27
Tweets, viewing, 5
Twitter
  connections, 67
  moral/political words, usage, 99
  posting, 102
  responses, 96

U
UFOs, videos/confirmation, 68
User engagement, metrics
  (display), 21

V
Variable rewards schedule, 42–43
Venus of Willendorf, 143
Video
  transmission, ease, 76
  watch time, amount (average),
    24–25
Viewers
  bias, cable news channels
    (appeal), 23
  desensitization, 27
  engagement time, 25
Virtual assistants, popularity (rise), 32

W
Web 3.0, changes,
  155–156
Weigel, Moira, 55
Well-being, factors, 90
Williams, James, 138
Wood, Wendy, 52
Working memory, demands,
  15–16
Worry, experience, 78

Y
Year of Outrage (*Slate*), 98
Yes man (metaphor), 68–69
YouTube
  algorithms, video
    recommendations,
    160–161
  content
    responsibility, 152
    user knowledge, 158
  legal protection, 151
  objective, 161–162
  subscribers, 68
  videos, viewing, 5, 160

Z
Zuckerberg, Mark, 153